SWEEPERS, SNAGS, AND STEAM

THE STEAMBOAT ERA ON MONTANA'S MISSOURI RIVER

ED WOLFF

RIVERBEND
PUBLISHING

Contents

Preface

ALTHOUGH I PURSUED A CAREER in veterinary medicine, I have been a serious student of history my entire life. The scope of my interests are varied: military conflicts, North American Indians, fur trade on the Northwest frontier and the accoutrements and survival strategies of the trappers ranging over the Rocky Mountains. Joe Meek, Jim Bridger, and Jedediah Smith were among the more notable of a unique breed of daring men with a proclivity to transcend the next horizon.

Having taken up residence in Montana 37 years ago, my interests bend toward the rich, tumultuous, history of the state. After reading an essay recounting the chronological record of significant events that occurred during the era of steamboat traffic on the Missouri River (1811 until 1890 spans the most important time during the development of the northwest frontier) and the impact the steam-powered craft had on the settlement of the Northwest, I wanted to learn more. The temerity of boat pilots/captains and crew members, boat design and operation, types of cargos, and the tenuous existence of wood hawks were subjects about which I wanted to learn more. What were the reasons for the demand of steamboat traffic? How were, or were not, the extreme hazards of river travel overcome? Hazards included hostile natives, turbulent currents, hidden sandbars, submerged trees capable of disemboweling a boat, violent headwinds and tornadoes, clouds of mosquitoes, collapsing riverbanks, and the ever present fear of boiler explosions and fires. Each spring huge volumes of opaque, muddy water, generated by spring snow melt, gouged new channels, eroded existing sandbars and raised new ones, rearranged submerged trees, sculpted new shoals and rapids and voided the previous year's mental maps stored in the minds of captains. The tortuous, winding course of the "Big Muddy" had to be relearned each season. A steamboat captain was responsible for tons of expensive cargo and the lives of the crew and passengers. His ability to "read" the capricious nature of the river required exceptional skills.

I began to gather information from a variety of sources: libraries, museums, magazine articles, newspaper articles, and obscure publications. To gain firsthand knowledge of Fort Benton and the Missouri, I floated and camped 140 miles of the river, launching at Fort Benton and ending at Kipp's Landing. Before beginning, I walked the levee that restrains the volatile Missouri from washing into the streets of Fort Benton. I studied several historically informative signs and enjoyed a stroll along the first bridge to span the Missouri in Montana. While camped on the bank of the muddy Missouri near the exact location where Meriwether Lewis wrote the words 208 years ago, I read passages from the "Definitive Journals of the Lewis and Clark Expedition." I gained an intimate perspective of the men themselves and the the Corps of Discovery's impact on the subsequent development of the western frontier via the sinuous artery of the Missouri.

A priceless treasure trove of intimate, detailed information has been left behind in the records of the American and Rocky Mountain fur companies, in the logs of steamboat captains, in the journals of literate passengers, in oral accounts, and from nearly 300,000 artifacts salvaged mid-20th century from the

Bertrand, a steamboat swallowed by the Missouri in 1865. These sources give firsthand, informative views of life on the Missouri River via steamboats during the 19th century.

Ed Wolff

Author's Note: Typically on large Mississippi River steamboats, the captain managed the business affairs of the boat while the pilot was responsible for navigation. On the smaller boats of the Upper Missouri, they were usually the same person. For the purposes of variety, I have used the terms interchangeably, but meaning the same, most senior person responsible for the operation of a steamboat. Steamboats may be described a steamboats, steamers, vessels, or boats. A steamer's freight may be described as freight, cargo, merchandise, or goods. Misspelled words and punctuation errors within the quotations of eyewitnesses are retained in respect for historical value and a sense of living vicariously through the speaker or author.

Paddlewheel steamboats plied the Upper Missouri River in the mid and late 1800s, delivering tons of goods and thousands of passengers upstream and taking million-dollar shipments of furs, hides, and gold downstream. In this photograph from 1877, the steamboat Helena *is moored at Cow Island, a steamboat landing during low water, 127 miles downstream from Fort Benton.*

Introduction

PROFITS WERE THE PRIME MOTIVATORS for attempting to conquer the Missouri River, causing entrepreneurs and adventurers to undertake the risks and dangers of traveling on the river. The riches of the American West—furs, buffalo hides, gold and other minerals, timber, agricultural land—were ripe for exploitation. An efficient, economical means to transport the wealth had to be found, and for a time, Missouri River steamboats were the means. Despite operating on a treacherous river and confined to a narrow window of time each year, hundreds of steamboats transported thousands of tons of cargo and thousands of passengers to the frontier, and then took millions of dollars of extracted natural resources down river to eastern and world markets.

Ambitious men seeking their fortunes or a new start in the virgin wilderness endured the perilous 2,300 mile journey from St. Louis to Fort Benton, Montana, the upper limits of steamboat navigation. The Upper Missouri (South Dakota, North Dakota, and Montana) was a vast swath of country uninhabited by descendants of European colonists. It was a land shrouded in rumor and mystery, populated by little-known native tribes, teaming with dangerous animals, and sculpted by a harsh, unforgiving climate.

The men—and some women—trusting their fate to the skill of a riverboat pilot and his crew represented an eclectic intermingling of nineteenth-century Americans: trappers, fur buyers, miners, rivermen, whiskey traders, adventurers,

Steamboats for the Upper Missouri were smaller than their grand counterparts on the Mississippi River. The "mountain boats" averaged 190 to 200 feet long. But the Montana, *shown here in 1879 during its only landing at Fort Benton, was immense. At 283 feet long and boasting two full-length decks, it was the largest steamboat to reach that far up the Missouri. In 1884 the* Montana *hit a railroad bridge in Missouri and sank, her career only lasting five years.* Archives and Special Collections, Mansfield Library, University of Montana.

artists, preachers, horse thieves, outlaws, soldiers, sportsmen, gamblers, soiled doves, and con men. Most were driven by greed and profit. A few were motivated by a sense of adventure. A number of educated travelers with discriminating tastes dared the perils of the river to paint, study, and observe.

Some of these fortune seekers would accumulate great wealth and return home as successful businessmen; some would return broke and disillusioned; a few would settle and tame the wilderness; many would leave their bones on the prairie.

This book describes the height of the steamboat era on the Upper Missouri River, a period from 1850 to 1889. It describes how the motives of early explorers and trappers influenced the development of steam-powered vessels; how ambition, greed, and "Manifest Destiny" ultimately influenced the maturation of steamboat traffic; and how the steamboat era impacted Native American cultures.

The book will also describe the steamboat industry: the boats and their designs, the captains and crews, the freight carried upstream and downstream, the financial risks and rewards, and the hazards and peculiarities of navigating the Missouri River.

To give the reader a sense of walking in the shoes of Native Americans and the men and women of European heritage who challenged the frontier, the text is liberally sprinkled with eyewitness accounts that provide firsthand descriptions of frontier experiences.

CHAPTER 1

Anatomy of the Missouri River

THE MISSOURI RIVER—nicknamed "Big Muddy," "Big Mo," or "Old Misery"—begins life in the remote recesses of the northern Rocky Mountains. Three rivulets, separated by mountain ranges and generated by melting snowfields, course downhill, their journeys ending at the Gulf of Mexico. Countless creeks and streams add to the coalescing flow until three major rivers are born. The Madison River, named in honor of James Madison who was Presidents Jefferson's Secretary of State and president of the United States from 1809 to 1817, originates in a remote corner of Yellowstone National Park and flows 133 miles to its juncture with the Jefferson River near Three Forks, Montana. The Gallatin River, the most rapid of the three, named for President Jefferson's Secretary of the Treasury, also originates in Yellowstone National Park, flowing 100 miles north through scenic valleys to add its volume to the Missouri River. The Jefferson River is generated by the confluence of the Big Hole, Ruby, and Beaverhead rivers. The Jefferson River drains the largest area, flowing 83 miles to blend with the Gallatin and Madison rivers, forming the massive Missouri River.

From its birth at Three Forks, Montana, the serpentine course of the Missouri flows in a generally northern direction, roughly paralleling the eastern front of the Rockies until reaching Great Falls, Montana, where the channel turns northeasterly, arcing to within 40 miles of the Canadian border. Paralleling the Canadian border, the river reaches Williston, North Dakota, where it turns south into South Dakota. Continuing south, the river defines the borders of Iowa, Nebraska, Kansas, and Missouri. At Kansas City the river swings east to join the Mississippi River just north of St. Louis, the Missouri's abrasive turbulence having carved a 2,546-mile swath through a varied landscape. Along its course the Missouri is fed by an enormous web of tributaries, gaining strength like an insatiable glutton and draining half a million square miles of five states. Together, these 20,000 miles of sinewy, web-like watery fingers opened overland routes into the heart of the West.

During its mercurial, downhill run to the Mississippi, the Missouri covers a distance longer than the entire length of the Mississippi, draining a watershed of 580,000 square miles. Its annual discharge is estimated to be 20 cubic miles of water; this represents a flow rate of 94,000 cubic feet per second, more than twice the volume of water from the upper Mississippi watershed.

The area through which the Missouri flows is known as the Missouri River Basin. Its volume and energy is increased exponentially because of major rivers—the Yellowstone, Marias, Bighorn, Powder, Tongue, and Platte Rivers—as well as uncountable lesser rivers, creeks, and streams. During the months of May and June, all tributaries flowing into the Missouri are swollen with snowmelt, greatly affecting the ability to navigate upstream against a 6- to 10-mile-per-hour current. However, as summer heat dissolves mountain and plains snowfields, water levels begin to fall, exposing numerous sandbars, sunken logs, and gravel shoals, making navigation by keelboats and steamboats extremely hazardous if not impossible.

Like an angry serpent, the river twists and turns as it searches for avenues of least resistance, scouring and reshaping landscapes, sweeping trees, brush, and debris before its implacable force. The unrelenting current collapses banks and gouges new channels, depositing huge amounts of mud and silt and giving the water a brown color. At intervals, topography has a way of slowing Big Muddy's flow. River bends tame the sinuous currents, settling tons of sediment and building new sandbars. One ambitious river traveler counted 173 river bends in Montana alone. The acuteness of some U-shaped bends create necks of land requiring several miles of river to navigate around, while land traverses of a few hundred yards across the bends would reach the same place in less time.

The enormous volume of water, reluctant to be contained or restrained, continually undercuts the river's banks, and over time, often happening without warning, the torrent will weaken a high bank, causing hundreds of cubic yards of earth, accompanied with uprooted trees and brush, to slough into the river, crushing anything in its path. The fear of a major accident weighed heavily on Captain Meriwether Lewis during the Lewis and Clark Expedition. In June 1804, about 350 miles above the mouth of the Missouri, Lewis wrote: "Set out this morning at an early hour, the courant strong; and the river very crooked; the banks are falling very fast; I sometimes wonder that some of our canoes or pirogues are not swallowed up by means of these immense masses of earth which are eternally precipitating themselves into the river; we have many hair breath escapes from them but providence seems so to have ordered it that we have as yet sustained no loss in consequence of them." (*Journals of Lewis and Clark*, Vol. 2)

Pierre-Antione Tabeau, an educated French-Canadian trader, living among the Arikara in the years 1803-1804, reported: "Some voyageurs who had camped in a high, wooded cover, not realizing that underneath it was being undermined by the current, believed that they were quite safe at the very moment that the banks crumbled, sweeping away in their fall the trees which engulfed the cargo and the boat."

The continual scouring of the river channel, the eroding and undercutting of banks, and the washing away of debris causes the river to shape the topography, often in remarkable ways. The softest of the sedimentary layers erode. Harder sediments, more resistant to erosive forces, leave a lunar landscape of arches, spires, hoodoos, and mushroom rocks (pillars of sediments capped by hard, weather-resistant rocks). Early French and English explorers called these unique geological regions the "Badlands."

On Friday, May 31, 1805, Meriwether Lewis had a different perspective as he passed the White Cliffs of the Missouri in present-day Chouteau County, Montana: "The hills and river Cliffs which we passed today exhibit a most romantic appearance. The bluffs of the river rise to the height of from 2 to 300 feet and in most places nearly perpendicular; they are formed of remarkable white sandstone which is sufficiently soft to give way readily to the impression of water....The water in the course of time in descending from those hills and plains on either side of the river has trickled down the soft sand cliffs and worn it into a thousand grotesque figures, which with the help of a little imagination and an oblique view at a distance, are made to represent elegant ranges of lofty freestone buildings, having their parapets well stocked with statuary; columns of various sculpture both grooved and plain, are also seen supporting long galleries in front of those buildings; in other places on

The rugged beauty of the Missouri Breaks in Montana has long inspired wonder and fanciful names. Here the Helena *is moored below the aptly named Steamboat Rock (date unknown).* MONTANA HISTORICAL SOCIETY RESEARCH CENTER PHOTOGRAPH ARCHIVES, HELENA, MONTANA.

a much nearer approach and with the help of less imagination we see the remains or ruins of elegant buildings; some columns standing and almost entire with their pedestals and capitals; others retaining their pedestals but deprived by time or accident of their capitals, some lying prostrate an broken others in the form of vast pyramids of conic structure bearing a series of other pyramids on their tops becoming less as they ascend and finally terminating in a sharp point. niches and alcoves of various forms and sizes are seen at different heights as we pass." (*Journals of Lewis and Clark,* Vol. 4)

The early traders who followed Lewis and Clark may not have felt the same way about the scenery, but they knew that at the end of a long winter, the Indians in the Missouri Basin were desperate to trade peltries for guns, powder, ammunition, blankets, knives, and trinkets. So the snowmelt-swollen Missouri, although a serious barrier, presented the most practical means to reach the tribes. As Pierre-Antione Tabeau noted about the risks: "Notwithstanding all the prudence and the foresight possible, these accidents cannot always be prevented; for, even while traveling, one is often obliged to face such risks for lack of other routes."

CHAPTER 2

Indian Nations of the Upper Missouri

IT HAS BEEN ESTIMATED that more than a dozen Indian nations inhabited the Upper Missouri River between the Blackfeet in Montana and the Arikara in South Dakota. Several tribes inhabited the lower Missouri River, the country from the Platte River in Nebraska downstream to St. Louis. In June 1804, Lewis and Clark, while ascending the lower Missouri, described the country the tribes inhabited: "I went out about 4ms. And found the country for one mile back good land and well watered the hills not high with a gentle assent form the river, well timbered with oak, walnut Hickory ash, &c. the land further back the Plains, Commence," (*Journals of Lewis and Clark,* Vol. 2)

The Osage and Missouri tribes inhabited the present-day state of Missouri; the Kansa people were a small tribe residing on the Kansas River. Their livelihoods depended on agriculture and hunting buffalo. The Poncas, once a thriving, well-populated, warlike nation, cultivated crops and hunted deer, turkeys, and small game. Because traders suffered theft and physical abuse while attempting to exchange goods with the Poncas for beaver and deer pelts, the traders avoided them. The tribe, for want of trade guns and powder, suffered from their enemies who had acquired them.

The Oto and Pawnee peoples roamed the Great Plains of Nebraska in the vicinity of the Platte River. Because the Pawnee were farmers as well as hunters, they belonged to the permanent village tribes. The principle crops were corn, squash, and pumpkins. Like the nomadic, tepee-dwelling tribes further west, the Pawnee were predatory and feared by most of the surrounding tribes. The tribe did a brisk business trading buffalo robes to traders. Early in the fur trade, buffalo robes were shipped down the Platte River in primitive bull boats, then, at the Missouri River, transferred to canoes destined for St. Louis.

The Sioux, Cheyenne, Arikara, Mandan, Crow, Blackfeet, and Gros Ventres were powerful and war-like buffalo-hunting tribes in the Upper Missouri. With the exception of the Arikara, Mandan, and Hidatsa, these tribes were nomadic, following the migrating buffalo herds across the Northern Plains.

The introduction of the horse and gun radically altered the cultures of all the tribes in the Missouri River basin. Possession and mastery of both greatly affected the balance of power among the tribes.

The strength and vitality of all the tribes depended on the consumption of large quantities of meat, primarily buffalo, supplemented with elk, deer, and antelope. In times of scarcity and frequent famines, the agriculturalists managed best, surviving winters on beans, squash, and corn. Wandering tribes, out of necessity, harvested a variety of wild roots, a resource called upon to alleviate famine. A staple was the prairie turnip, a common, widely distributed tuber eaten raw or boiled. To preserve the turnip for long periods, it was cut into pieces and dried in the sun or pounded to a powder. The resulting flour was rich, nourishing, and palatable when made into a meat soup. Horses transported great quantities of the

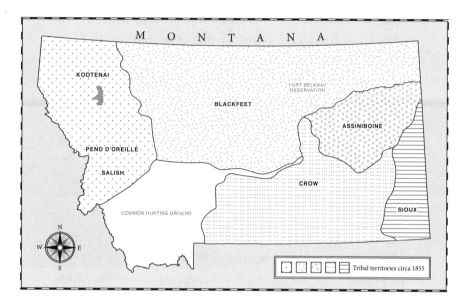

As the steamboat era began on the Upper Missouri, Indian nations occupied the entire area that later became Montana. This map shows the approximate tribal territories circa 1855. FROM MONTANA 1889, COURTESY RIVERBEND PUBLISHING.

pounded or dried roots to be bartered with the Arikara for corn and beans.

During the early 1800s, the Sioux Nation was divided into five principal tribes roaming a vast swath of land encompassing Nebraska, North and South Dakota. Anthropologists have estimated their population to number about 15,000 people. Over time the Teton and Yankton branches of the Sioux nation caused much havoc in the early years of the fur trade, being particularly aggressive to traders ascending the Missouri and later ambushing steamboats. The Sioux become known as the "pirates of the Missouri."

Buffalo-hunting nomads, the Blackfeet were an aggressive

tribe that controlled the High Plains from southern Alberta, Canada, south along the eastern flanks of the Rocky Mountains into Montana. The Blackfeet Nation numbered about 14,000 individuals, living in four distinct bands. Blackfeet men and women were physically fit, excelled at horsemanship, were bold in battle, and marked by showy extravagance. The men were fond of athletics, liquor, and gambling. In wagers of desperation, men would bet the clothes on their backs.

All the Blackfoot bands were predatory, existing in an ongoing state of warfare with other tribes and wandering over vast expanses of land. The Blackfeet controlled the richest beaver country in the Upper Missouri, but only the boldest trappers and traders dared enter this coveted region. The Gros Ventres Blackfeet were persistently hostile to the whites; any trapper crossing paths with them was in imminent danger of death. There is no historical record of how many trappers died lonely, violent deaths, their scalps becoming bloody trophies displayed on warriors' lodges, and their rifles, shot pouches, and personal effects taken as spoils of war.

Until the time of the Lewis and Clark Expedition (except for irregular and infrequent contact with French and Spanish traders), the Indian tribes of the Upper Missouri led lives of near constant struggle. Because the migration patterns of buffalo were unpredictable—driven by finding forage, water, and avoiding severe weather—famines frequently stalked the Indian villages. Tribes also lived in perpetual states of war and retaliation. Fear of attack was nearly constant. The Indians endured a fickle climate, suffered months of mind-numbing cold, sometimes survived only on dried meat or parched corn and dried squash, and were clothed only in leather, wrapped in a buffalo robe. These hardships had a debilitating effect. For these reasons the population of Indians in the Upper Missouri never amounted to more than a few tens of thousands, and for a long time very few whites were in the area. This all quickly changed after the Lewis and Clark Expedition.

CHAPTER 3

The Lewis and Clark Expedition

PRESIDENT THOMAS JEFFERSON commissioned Meriwether Lewis and William Clark to explore the potential of the newly acquired Louisiana Purchase, a swath of land that would more than double the size of the United States. The history of the Lewis and Clark Expedition is well known. Beginning in 1804, the "Corps of Discovery" made its way up the Missouri River, crossed the Rocky Mountains, and descended the Colombia River to the Pacific Ocean. After wintering on the coast, the band of explorers again crossed the Rockies, descended the Missouri River, and returned triumphant to St. Louis in 1806.

Whenever possible, the expedition used boats to travel and transport gear. Preparing for the expedition in 1803, Lewis went to Pittsburgh to supervise the construction of a 55-foot-long keelboat. The specially designed flat-bottomed boat would transport the lifeblood of the expedition up the unmapped Missouri. It would be the first boat capable of carrying more than a ton of cargo to penetrate the Upper Missouri.

On May 14, 1804, the men in high spirits, the Lewis and Clark Expedition left winter camp on the Dubois River in present-day Illinois. The group consisted of about 40 men with a heavily laden keelboat and two pirogues (boat-like canoes). It quickly became apparent that bucking the current and navigating obstacles, while pushing up the Missouri during spring run-off, was a slow and laborious process. Progress included poling, or men on shore pulling the boats with a tow rope, or infrequent sailing with a favorable wind. Towing from shore required mental discipline and extreme physical effort. Often above their waists in water, the men fought sucking mud, sandbars, logs and brush, and clouds of mosquitoes. The unremitting toil sapped energy; to fuel their bodies, each man consumed seven to eight pounds of meat per day when available.

When the Missouri became too shallow and swift for the keelboat, the expedition built canoes from cottonwood trees and took them farther into the headwaters of the river. After crossing the Rocky Mountains on foot and horseback, the group used canoes to descend the Columbia River. On the return journey, canoes again were used.

The importance of the Lewis and Clark expedition cannot be overemphasized. From the outset its success was unpredictable, its potential staggering. It were as if the men were going to the moon. At first, the Indians thought the whites were members of a strange, weak tribe of little consequence. In reality, the expedition was the vanguard of an overwhelming inundation of whites. Reports of vast forests, vast mineral deposits, multiple millions of acres of arable land, and fur and game resources of unlimited potential eventually drew tens of thousands of fortune seekers: trappers, traders, miners, land speculators, homesteaders, industrialists, and the accompanying riffraff. Lewis and Clark recognized the potential of their discoveries, often commenting in their journals on the future colonization of the fertile bottom lands and the extraction of natural resources.

The subsequent competition for the bounty of furs and profits in the western wilderness would have a profound effect on native peoples, deplete animal populations, and bring serious competition to British inholdings in the northwest. The Lewis and Clark Expedition had crossed a continent, charting the course and character of the Missouri River for the steamboats that would bring to fruition the concept of Manifest Destiny. (At the time, the confiscation of Indian lands and settling the tribes on reservations was an accepted practice in U.S. nation building.)

CHAPTER 4

Fur Trappers and Traders

AT FIRST THE WEST'S WEALTH was furs, especially beaver. The beaver's soft, waterproof underfur, known as "muffoon," is webbed with tiny barbs that when shaved makes a soft sheet of felt. The processed felt was attached to top hats worn by men of means and fashion in Europe.

The dribble of white traders and trappers that began after the Lewis and Clark Expedition soon turned into a flood, and fantastic trade goods rapidly raised the standard of living of the tribes. The manufactured goods supplied by the whites in exchange for furs and robes included wool blankets, steel knives, metal cooking pots, firearms, clothing, sugar, salt, flour, liquor, and an endless supply of mirrors, copper wire, beads, and other trinkets. The Indians' way of life quickly became dependent on the acquisition of these goods, fundamentally changing their

Beaver fur was the first major export from the Upper Missouri. The felt was made into fashionable top hats like this one for the upper class in England and elsewhere. The beaver trade launched the surge of Anglo-Europeans into the region.

cultures. At the same time, nothing was more morally degrading to the Indians as a people than whiskey, and introduced European diseases proved much worse, nearly exterminating several tribes. This combination of factors destroyed the fabric of native societies. The exploitation of the tribes began simply enough, but it inexorably led to their near extinction.

During the spring and fall, entire Indian villages would camp in the immediate proximity of strategically positioned trading posts and forts (fort was a loosely used word to describe a small, crudely constructed log structure or a strongly fortified, well-constructed building) to trade furs and buffalo robes for necessities.

Forts such as Fort McKenzie on the Upper Missouri in Montana were constructed with security as a priority. Stout, straight pine logs, placed vertically in the ground, formed walls enclosing square or rectangular areas. Inside Fort McKenzie and against the exterior walls were constructed workshops, warehouses, and living quarters. These ancillary rooms formed the walls of a corridor leading to the main entrance gate built of heavy timbers that could be securely barred.

A second gate closed the interior of the corridor, preventing access to the interior of the fort. In the walls of the corridor were heavily barred windows that could be opened to facilitate trade. Indians were admitted only in small groups and only when well-armed men provided security. After the interior gate was secured, a pushing, shouting crowd, burdened with furs and robes, entered through the opened front gate. After admitting eight to ten individuals, or as many as seemed prudent, the exterior gate was closed to the vociferous protests of the excluded. Most trade was conducted from the warehouse window. The sales agent not only had to control the jostling customers, he had to be well versed in bargaining for the best possible exchange rates for his goods. The task demanded the skills of a diplomat to mollify often indignant customers not satisfied with the exchange rate.

The skins of fox, wolf, martin, and other peltries played an insignificant role in the peltry trade; buffalo robes and beaver skins were the principle units of commerce. Buffalo robes were taken to trading posts located in reasonable proximity to a tribe's home range. The Indians learned that the value of a robe could be divided among any number of goods, depending on the needs of the customer. Half a robe's value could be exchanged for coffee and flour, or sugar and cotton cloth, or tobacco and whiskey. This made the trading exchange efficient and understandable.

On a good day, hundreds of robes could be exchanged for articles that had become indispensable. A woman burdened with quantities of robes weighing multiple pounds would wait patiently outside the log trading house. She, led by her husband, entered the building and threw the robes over the counter one by one. He would then point to the desired items: one robe traded for 3 cups of coffee, or six cups of sugar, or 10 cups of flour; 6 or more robes bought a gun or a saddle; a three-point Mackinaw blanket cost three robes. Beads, bells, ribbons, cloth, and other fancy items afforded the most handsome profits because they were inexpensive and less cumbersome to transport from the East. Pale blue necklace beads used for personal decoration and embroidering clothing were highly sought by the Indians. Although prohibited by laws,large profits could be made selling whiskey to the Indians. Enforcement of such laws at the remote trading posts was non-existent.

Prior to 1831, because of the belligerent nature of the Blackfeet, no trading post had been erected above the mouth of the Yellowstone River. In October of that year James Kipp erected Fort Piegan—in honor of the Piegan band of Blackfeet—on the left bank of the Missouri a short distance above the mouth of the Marias River in north-central Montana. The following spring Kipp abandon the post, and the Indians burned it down. In 1832 Fort McKenzie, another trading post built on the Missouri above the confluence of the Marias, established a profitable trade with the Blackfeet until the winter of 1843. Mr. Chardon, chief trader at the fort reported, "...the Blackfeet are getting more and more troublesome in consequence of certain retrenchments of liquor heretofore given them in their ceremonies, the discontinuation of which has become absolutely necessary for the continuation of the post." Chardon, unable to safely leave the post more than once a week, abandoned the structure in the spring of 1843. The Blackfeet promptly burned it down.

From 1550 until 1840, beaver felt hats were stylish. (In 1760 the Hudson's Bay Company exported to England enough North American beaver pelts to make 576,000 hats). Because of long transportation routes, limited supply, and the complicated, expensive process of hat making, only the rich could afford a beaver top hat. Initially, a prime pelt fetched $6 (about $115 in today's dollars), but by the early 1840s, because of changing fashion, the price of a prime pelt had collapsed to $2. Silk hats had replaced beaver hats. Though the beaver era on the Upper Missouri lasted only 30 years (from 1810 to 1840), it was the free-wheeling beaver men, braving a raw wilderness, trapping virgin waters, and risking their hair, that laid the bedrock for the evolution and maturation of steamboat commerce on the Upper Missouri.

When the beaver trade collapsed, buffalo hides became the principle commodity of exchange until the immense herds of buffalo were nearly exterminated by intense hunting. Animals were replaced by mineral (primarily gold), timber, and land exploitation. The nature of the terrain and the quantities of resources destined the Missouri River to become the artery of commerce.

CHAPTER 5

Artists, Naturalists, and Chroniclers

RUBBING ELBOWS WITH THE RAW-BONED adventurers in the Upper Missouri were a number of educated, talented, and well-bred men who saw value in experiencing and recording the unique and fast disappearing wilderness and natives of the American West. Eccentric naturalist-explorers, most of insufficient means to finance or organize an expedition, sought to attach themselves to fur companies or government-sponsored expeditions. They went to closely examine and record—in word and paint— the wildlife, plant life, Indians, and nature of the land.

Compiling a prodigious, accurate record of the customs and mannerisms of the native tribes became a life's mission for professionally trained artist George Catlin. In the spring of 1832 steamboat traffic on the Missouri had become somewhat common, and Catlin booked passage on the *Yellowstone*, a boat put into service by the American Fur Company to transport furs to St. Louis. Catlin's work regarding native culture is distinguished from his peers by his attention to detail: tepee design, stretched and dried scalps hanging from tent poles, postures of men reclining after suffering a raid gone awry, sketches of men mounted on snowshoes spearing buffalo wallowing in snow drifts, and a Sioux scalp dance.

Commissioned by the American Fur Company, the side-wheeler Yellowstone *(also written as* Yellow Stone*) was the first steamboat to reach Fort Union, a fur trading post near the confluence of the Yellowstone and Missouri rivers. The year was 1833. As the fur trade grew, companies looked for ways to speed up the transport of trade goods and furs. It was the birth of the steamboat era on the Upper Missouri.*

Prince Maximilian, a German aristocrat and explorer, took the steamboat Yellowstone *to Fort Union in 1833. He wanted to see and record the wilderness and the Native Americans before they were engulfed by Anglo-Europeans. Maximilian came with an entourage that included the Swiss painter Karl Bodmer, who was the first trained artist to make paintings of the Upper Missouri region.*

One naturalist-hunter not dependent on a patron was German-born Alexander Philip Maximilian, Prince of Wied. His credentials as a risk-taking adventurer were impressive. As a Major-General in the Napoleonic wars, he led a division in the capture of Paris. Released from the army, he conducted a prolonged expedition to South America, exploring Brazilian rain forests. He spent a decade meticulously recording the animal and plant life and completing a book of maps of the country.

Artist Karl Bodmer painted this scene of freight being off loaded from the steamboat Yellowstone, *stuck on a sandbar. After removing enough freight to free the boat, the freight would be loaded again upstream of the obstruction. Built in Louisville, Kentucky, in 1831, the* Yellowstone *was the first steamboat to navigate the Missouri River above Omaha, Nebraska.*

In 1832, fifty-year-old Prince Maximilian, aware of the rapidly changing landscape, sailed from Europe to the United States with a considerable retinue, including Swiss artist Karl Bodmer, fulfilling a desire to witness and scientifically record the pristine, unspoiled, American West. In April 1833, leaving St Louis, Maximilian and his entourage boarded the *Yellowstone* and began the 2,000-mile journey to Fort Union near the confluence of the Yellowstone River and about 490 miles downstream from where Fort Benton would later be built.

Bodmer had studied art in Paris and had developed a style that adapted well to recording the uniqueness of the indigenous wildlife and Indians in the Rocky Mountain region. His paintings portray in intimate details the native people's personal belongings: moccasins, weapons, and body decorations. His sketches and paintings of the sandstone spires of the Missouri River Breaks, and his paintings of wildlife, became pictorial evidence for a fledgling government anxious to lay claim to the entire continent.

In 1843, American artist and naturalist John James Audubon chose to take the same journey up the Missouri that Maximilian had taken ten years previously. Audubon was 58 years old and anxious to complete an illustrated work portraying the mammals and birds of the West. He took the American Fur Company's *Omega* to Fort Union.

CHAPTER 6

St. Louis, the Starting Point

DESPITE TALES ABOUT THE DANGERS, death, and hardships of life on the prairies and in the mountains, interest in the West gained momentum. Americans of all persuasions looked at the interior of the continent in new ways: gold discoveries promised great wealth, new settlements needed services—bankers, shop keepers, smithies, law enforcement, sawmills—and raw land beckoned homesteaders. To not a few, the simple promise of a fresh start was motive enough to leave the old life and embark on an adventure with no known end.

The passion to populate the west to the shores of the Pacific became known as America's Manifest Destiny. The highway to fulfill that promise was the Missouri River, and the vehicles to travel that highway were steamboats.

St. Louis, located on the western bank of the Mississippi River just below the mouth of the Missouri, was in an advantageous location. By 1830, the city had gradually become the epicenter of western expansion. From its docks, steamboats by the dozens transported men and supplies 2,300 miles to Fort Benton, Montana. All manner of goods—flour, salt, sugar, metals, arms and ammunition, clothing, and tools—were off loaded by stevedores. Tons of beaver pelts and buffalo robes, stored in crude warehouses, were loaded on board

THE LEVEE AT ST LOUIS, MISSOURI.—Photographed by R. Benecke, St. Louis.—[See Page 527.]

In the 1800s St. Louis was the hub for steamboats operating throughout the interior of the United States, including on the Mississippi, Missouri, Ohio, and several other rivers. This illustration shows steamboats on the St. Louis levee as far as the eye can see. The levee was six miles long and could serve 170 boats at once. Most steamboats for the Upper Missouri left St. Louis in March and April to catch spring runoff on the upper river. Runoff provided deeper water over sandbars and rocky shoals.

for the tedious return trip to St. Louis. By 1830, $3,750,000 worth of peltries had reached the city.

The city continued to be a depot for all manner of goods from the East destined for the frontier. Streets, although poorly maintained, were surveyed. Quays were constructed to accommodate burgeoning steamboat traffic. Entrepreneurs built saloons, hotels, restaurants, and stores to accommodate an influx of farrago humanity with diverse motives.

Attracted by profits in gambling, prostitution, scams, and trading liquor to the Indians, the usual rabble followed. Taverns sprung up along the riverfront where rivermen, trappers (recently arrived from the interior), ex-soldiers, and drifters met to drink, womanize, gamble, and fight. Lacking law enforcement until after 1838, crime in the city's underbelly was uncontrolled. Thieves and muggers roamed unchallenged. Above the debauchery, St. Louis presented a different face. Elite, wealthy fur merchants, anxious to monitor their financial interests, competed with one another in constructing lavish homes and furnishing them with imported woods and crystal. The well-to-do sponsored lively social events, providing employment for musicians and caterers. A mayor and a city council were elected, and by 1840, the population of St. Louis counted 16,000 individuals.

Until the end of the steamboat era, St. Louis remained the hub of western migration, especially during the big influx of homesteaders into the fertile valleys of Oregon and prospectors into the gold fields of California, Idaho, and Montana. Other river towns also became important embarkation ports for immigrants. Atchison, St. Joseph, Independence, and Council Bluffs were all destinations for overland travelers who outfitted for trips to California and the Rocky Mountain region. In 1860, 60 steamers were making 300 calls to points of departure. Steamboats transported mining gear, livestock, small wagons, farm implements, and the clothing and personal items of men, women, and children—all the necessities to start lives on the frontier.

CHAPTER 7

Bull Boats to Keelboats

OVER TIME, THE TYPES OF CRAFTS that navigated the mercurial waters of the Missouri River changed according to advances in technology, changing cargos, volume of water, and destinations.

The Indians had devised a boat of shallow draft, easily maneuvered, and capable of safely navigating the vagarious waters of the Missouri. The ingenious craft, known as a "bull boat," was capable of carrying heavy loads of people and freight and could be built quickly of readily available material. The frame of the boat was made of supple willow branches or any other pliable material that could be bent into a bowl shape. The bent branches crossed in the center at the bottom and were secured into one unit at the top with bark strips or lengths of sinews, forming a lip to the bowl. The boat would be three or four feet in diameter and 20 inches deep. Buffalo hides, either green hides from a fresh kill or dry ones that were well soaked in water, were stretched tightly over the willow frame, with the hair to the inside. If green hides were used, the completed boat was dried over a low fire, shrinking and hardening the hides, making a snug, tight fit. Any seams were caulked with buffalo fat.

Once dried, the boat was durable, waterproof, and could be easily carried and launched by a woman. The buoyant tub

The first watercraft on the Upper Missouri were "bull boats" crafted by Native Americans. Built by stretching buffalo hides across a bowl-shaped frame of willow branches (top photo), the boats were fairly quick to make, carried hundreds of pounds, and easily dismantled when no longer needed. The boats were propelled by one person (bottom photo), usually a woman, making sculling strokes with a single paddle. Trappers sometimes used bull boats to transport furs downstream. Top photo, State Historical Society of North Dakota; bottom photo, Library of Congress.

was usually paddled by a woman. Kneeling at the front of the boat—as determined by the direction of travel—she made a paddling motion directly under the boat, expertly advancing the unwieldy craft by using an oscillating, side-to-side motion with each stroke of the paddle.

Groups of men and women would travel on land some distance up the Missouri to intercept a migrating herd of buffalo. After harvesting them, bull boats could be made from materials at hand and covered with fresh buffalo hides. The meat being loaded, groups of one or two dozen boats, each propelled with remarkable ease by a single person, paddled the boats back to the village. These practiced sailors safely navigated the unstable crafts through considerable winds, waves, and crosscurrents.

Bull boats had one serious flaw. As the day wore on, the skins would become waterlogged, making the boats less manageable. Time had to be taken to beach the boat, unload the cargo, build a fire, and dry the boat by continually rotating it before the fire, exposing it evenly to the flames.

Although the skin boat had limited range, it efficiently transported meat, furs, and people. They were utilitarian, needing a scant four inches of water to transport three men or several hundred pounds of meat across the Missouri.

Although the earliest trappers and traders were familiar with bull boats, Captain Lewis penned the first description of the crafts. Sgt. Nathaniel Pryor, (a member of the expedition) while pursuing a planned rendezvous with Captain Clark, led a group of men overland to the Yellowstone River. There, in an unguarded moment, a band of Crows slipped into camp under the cover of darkness and stole the group's horses. The men, having studied the techniques of the Indians, built bull boats and floated a considerable distance to successfully rejoin Captain Clark.

Bull boats continued to be a reliable means of transporting goods and people well into the steamboat era. Using a modified construction, white trappers would, in times of necessity, build a frame of willows in the shape of a crude canoe, then cover the structure with hides. The leaky, unstable craft transported men, furs, and trade goods on tributaries of the Missouri or on the Missouri proper.

In the spring of 1805, preparing to leave the Mandan village and ascend the Missouri to its source, Lewis and Clark sent their keelboat back to St. Louis. The captains instructed the remaining men to build six canoes from large cottonwood trees. The moisture-loving cottonwood was found along streams and riverbanks, growing to great heights and large diameters. The species is not ideal for canoe construction, but large trees were available and the wood easily worked. The tree trunks were cut in 14- to 20-foot sections and hollowed out using fires and adz work, and stabilized using cross braces. A skilled carpenter supervised the laborious construction. Loaded with cargo and manned by two or four men, the craft required skill and attention while paddling upstream against a significant current, dodging uprooted trees, and maneuvering around sandbars.

Needing a more stable craft to move the expedition forward, the captains ordered the construction of two pirogues. These specialized craft were floating platforms. Two canoes were lashed parallel to each other by two or more poles. The poles were then decked over with planks or small-diameter poles. The vessel was light, about 30-feet long, from 6- to 12-feet wide, and powered by 7 or 8 oars.

The pirogue had several advantages: a substantial amount of cargo could the efficiently transported, the craft was light and reasonably agile, and a small sheltered cabin/tent could be constructed on deck, providing some relief from sun, wind, and rain. A crude square sail fitted to the center of the craft provided occasional relief to the oarsmen. Using material at hand, the useful craft could be constructed quickly with minimal labor. There were serious disadvantages: a high profile made progress against the Missouri's frequent strong winds difficult, often requiring layovers, and swirling, whirlpool currents made the craft less manageable.

The keelboat specifically addressed the problems of transporting several tons of goods and large numbers of men up the Missouri. Its design was dictated by the river and the uses to which it would be applied. After a period of trial and error, most keelboats were built of the same pattern, differing only in length and width of beam. Keelboats were large, heavy crafts averaging about 55 feet in length, weighing an average of 10 tons. The wide beam was 16 to 18 feet. The boat's hulls were framed and planked with whip-sawed lumber, and a heavy keel ran the length of the bottom.

Well-built keelboats could carry about fifteen tons of cargo. The entire deck, except for short spaces fore and aft to allow the passage of a single person, was covered with a cargo box. The plank box stood about five-feet tall and had a waterproof roof. The box sheltered thousands of dollars of merchandise, constituting the heart of the vessel. Sixteen-inch-wide walkways ran along on both sides of the cargo box, fore and aft. Wood or metal slats fastened to the floor of the walkway provided stable footing.

There were four methods to advance a keelboat against the unrelenting current of the Missouri. A mast amid ship could be fitted with a square sail. If a vigorous wind blew against the stern, the sail could move the boat upstream, much to the joy of the oarsmen. Wind strength, duration, and direction

With their larger size and enclosed cargo holds, keelboats increased the volume of trade goods and furs shipped on the Upper Missouri. Heavily built with a stout keel and long rudder, they were rowed, pushed, pulled, and sailed upstream. In the top sketch, crew members are "poling," or pushing the boat upstream with long poles. When a pushing crewman reached the stern of the boat, he quickly raced to the bow to start pushing again. In the bottom sketch, the keelboat is being "cordelled," or pulled upstream by crewmen on the river bank using a long, thick rope. When the river bank was not passable, the men would wade in the water, fighting deep drop-offs, slick rocks, and sinking mud.

continually changed with every twist and turn of the channel, making use of wind propulsion unpredictable. When lucky, half a day's respite would be granted the laboring men.

Poling the boat demanded near super-human physical exertion and the nimbleness of a cat. It was a complicated task. Poles, all long, varied in length according to the height and strength of the boatmen. For better control, one end of the pole was fitted with a ball that fit under a man's armpit. Facing the stern, an equal number of men lined up on the narrow walkway on each side of the central cargo box. The men would plant the tip of their poles in the river bottom, securing it by "feel" with imperceptible skill. Setting the poles on slippery rocks, loose mud, or tangled snags would throw the men off balance and out of rhythm, possibly tipping the boatmen into the river. With balls securely snuggled into shoulders, the men would bend nearly horizontal and in unison, feet gripping the cleated floor, trudge aft, inching the laden boat forward. Reaching aft, each man would disengage his pole, run to the bow and reset the pole before the current nullified their work. To the uninitiated, feeling the bottom with their poles, finding solid sets, leaning into the poles, laboring aft, and returning quickly to the bow to reset poles appeared as a choreographed dance. In truth, using pole power to advance a keelboat against the Missouri's current demanded coordinated finesse and extreme physical conditioning.

When the water depth or a muddy bottom prohibited the use of poles, the keelboat moved forward by six or more oarsmen to a side. Again, rowing demanded serious, backbreaking labor. To keep the boat's bow pointed in the correct direction, the cadence of six to twelve oarsmen had to be synchronized. Rowing could be hazardous. Logs, branches, and assorted debris pushed along by the current could snap an oar, driving the jagged shaft into the rower's body with killing force. The captain of the vessel stood on the cargo box at the stern of the boat. From the elevated perch, he scouted the river for obstructions, shouting instructions to an experienced rudder man, who hand-operated a massive rudder affixed to a long, hand-held pole. Implicit understanding and cooperation between the captain and rudder man steered the boat away from disasters.

The cordelle provided another reliable way to inch the keelboat upstream, but it exposed the men to grievous injury and extreme privation. The technique involved as many as 26 men pulling on a thick rope up to 1,000 feet long to advance a fully loaded, ten-ton, awkward boat upstream yard by yard.

The shore of the Missouri was miserable beyond description. The cordellers waded through waist-deep mud, chest-deep water, stumbled across crumbling clay banks and sloping rocks, and scrambled through underbrush that ripped flesh and clothes like barbed wire. They fell, rolled, and wallowed in quicksand. They cursed at a rope that tangled on snags, rocks, and fallen trees. Hoards of choking, buzzing mosquitoes erupted from disturbed brush. Each man hosted a personal cloud of the black insects.

The labor was as toilsome as men had ever done anywhere. It is hard to understand how a French boatman, for weeks, sustained his exertions on a diet of fried corn for breakfast, fat pork and biscuits the consistency and shape of a hockey puck for the noon meal, and a bowl of a greasy, meatless slurry containing a pound of tallow (fat) for supper. Occasionally, a merciful captain provided dried fruit or flour. At night, shelter from the frequent rains, stiff winds, cold, and clouds of mosquitoes consisted of a tiny tent made by throwing a blanket over brush or a low hanging limb. Every night hosts of blood-sucking wood ticks would be plucked from bruised skin. Yet, the men persevered.

When the nature of the terrain made cordelling impossible, "warping" substituted. The rope, anchored to a solid snag or tree upstream from the boat, was hauled in by men on the keelboat, moving the boat upstream. The process was repeated as often as necessary. Not uncommonly, all four tactics of creeping the laden keelboat upstream were used in a single day. Going upstream, keelboats averaged six to eight miles per day, about the same distance later wagon trains would cover in a day.

Why would men of good sense become boatmen? Recognizing the destructive effects of liquor traded to the Indians, the United States government prohibited all liquor trade and its transport up river, but an exception was made for the rivermen. Four ounces of liquor per day for the length of the voyage induced an unending supply of applicants. In addition, each keelboat had a compliment of hunters with the express duty of supplying meat; buffalo, the preferred fare, was supplemented with antelope, deer, elk, and beaver. Quality exempted, the majority of the boatmen enjoyed steady rations for the first time. Four ounces of liquor per day and a full belly was more than the roughhewn, uneducated boatmen had known, a fare exchange for their labors.

For downriver transport of furs, some traders eschewed keelboats for flat-bottomed Mackinaws. These boats were built along the Upper Missouri of hand-sawed lumber, usually straight-grained pine. Fort Union and other forts had facilities, called chantiers, for building boats. Hand sawing boards from a pine log required considerable time and effort, indicative of the value of the fur cargos. The unpowered boats had pointed bows and square sterns that were held together

with wood dowels. They carried furs, a variety of other cargos, and 9 to 12 passengers, the total weighing up to 15 tons.
The 20- to 26-foot vessels drifted with the 6- to 10-mile-per-
hour current and were steered by stern-mounted, hand-held
rudders worked by experienced boatmen. Muscling 15-foot
oars, oarsmen would aid the rudder man, powering crafts
around obstacles. After floating 60 to 80 miles per day, boats
would moor at serviceable camp sites.

Mackinaws served their purpose perfectly, considering the
vessels had a scant 6 to 8 inches of freeboard. Their flat bottoms and shallow drafts passed over sandbars and rocky shoals,
avoiding punctured hulls. Traveling with the current, Mackinaws avoided many of the hazards coursing down the river and
were relatively easy to control. The 2,500-mile trip from Fort
Benton to St. Louis averaged 40 to 50 days. Upon reaching
their destinations, the boats were sold for $4 or $5 each and
ripped apart, the lumber used for firewood or construction.

Daily life on a keelboat, pirogue, or Mackinaw became a
repetition of the day before and a preview of the day to come,
with unforeseen adventures thrown in for excitement. The
captain of the vessel remained in constant anxiety. The deck
box held valuable cargo; its safe arrival rested squarely on the
captain's shoulders. He knew the river secreted deadly hazards to wrest it from his care. Taking precautions, a captain
chose a few keen-eyed, experienced men, their heads on swiv-
els, to stand in rotation at the bow. They were responsible for
detecting logs or whole trees plowing down the river. Giant
cottonwood trees, sprouting root balls and tangles of foot-
thick limbs, usually could be seen and avoided. More ominous were the "sawyers" lurking unseen beneath the murky
surface. These were submerged tree trunks with one end held
fast in the muddy bottom. The current whipped the free

ends in a violent oscillation that could rip open a boat's hull. The sickening crunching and snapping of hull timbers signaled the loss of cargo, boat, and maybe some crew. "Planters" were trees fixed to the bottom, stationary but deadly, poised to impale a hull. Waterlogged tree trunks floated downstream submerged just enough in the opaque water to be overlooked. Shoals and sandbars were floated over—until the boat grounded. A keelboat that swung broadside against the powerful current had little chance. Helpless, swept downriver, out of control, it risked being capsized.

Proof of such madness occurred in 1822. Bound for the mountains, the keelboat *Enterprise* departed St. Louis in May. Some 30 miles below the mouth of the Kansas River, disaster struck. Rounding a point, the mast struck an overhanging tree branch, swinging the boat broadside to the current. Swept into a maze of sawyers, their ends flashing up and down like jagged-toothed serpents, the *Enterprise's* hull was punctured and she sank, washing the $10,000 cargo and men into the river.

At night a boat's captain selected a level, dry site with a sufficient wood for a camp. Wounds were assuaged, the day's events discussed, repairs made, and meat cooked. Boatmen, satiated with pounds of protein, fell into an exhausted sleep. At dawn, it all started over again.

Each morning hunters were dispatched to walk the banks, scouring the surrounding country for game. Sometimes the passengers, weary of inching snail-like up river, would disembark to escape the confines of the boat. Investigating bankside curiosities relieved the tedium of upriver travel. Occasionally, naturalists would hitch a ride with trapping parties, content to collect unclassified species of plants and animals.

On a good day 12 miles of river could be gained, but 6 to

8 miles were more common. One fortunate boat made the trip from St. Louis to the Mandan village averaging 18 miles per day. The passage up the Missouri by keelboat averaged two or three months. The omnipresent sounds of the river never abated: the hiss of the silt-laden current; floating logs and limbs grinding and snapping; the current driving logs into cracking piles of driftwood; the current pulling apart the tangles to again set free floating hazards. These same dangers would soon bedevil steamboats.

CHAPTER 8

The Need for Steam

UNTIL ABOUT 1820 the bulk of supplies and trade goods destined for the intermountain west were carried to the Pacific Coast via ships called windjammers. These fast vessels, equipped with multiple sails, left New York City, sailed around the tip of South America, and up the coast to Oregon. Tons of supplies were off loaded, replaced by bales of furs. This valuable cargo, destined for London, New York, Canton, and other ports, made the weeks-long return voyage. As the trade grew, it became apparent that to harvest more furs—and make more profit—a more efficient, less costly means of getting trade goods to the tribes and trappers, and the furs out of the mountains, was required.

William H. Ashley entered the fur trade to make his fortune. He arrived in St. Louis in 1802, mindful of making money and entering politics. He conceived the novel idea of developing commerce in the fur business by transporting goods and necessities overland to the trappers who were stationed indefinitely in the mountains. The mountain men would be supplied with vital supplies: powder, lead, rifles and spare parts, rifle flints, traps, tobacco, whiskey, coffee, sugar, and ribbon and beads for their native women. Trade articles for the Indians included knives, rifles, lead, powder, steel arrowheads, kettles, blankets, blue beads, mirrors, whiskey, and

William H. Ashley was eager to make a fortune in the fur trade. He co-founded the Rocky Mountain Fur Company and created the annual rendezvous system, a boisterous summertime gathering of trappers, Indians, and pack trains filled with trade goods and supplies from the east. This rendezvous system lasted 15 years, from 1825 to 1840, until keelboats and steamboats forced their way up the Missouri.

traps. Tons of trade goods were transported by pack strings of horses and mules, animals sometimes numbering in the hundreds. The trappers, Indians, and supply train would meet at a prearranged location called a Rendezvous. The first one was in 1825, the last one in 1840.

The annual Rendezvous evolved into a business convenience to address the problems of supply and distribution. They also were rodeos of unparalleled excesses. Great hunts secured quantities of meat to feed hundreds. Trading booths

TO
Enterprising Young Men.

THE subscriber wishes to engage ONE HUN-
DRED MEN, to ascend the river Missouri
to its source, there to be employed for one, two
or three years.—For particulars, enquire of Major Andrew Henry, near the Lead Mines, in the
County of Washington, (who will ascend with,
and command the party) or to the subscriber at
St. Louis.

Wm. H. Ashley.

February 13   ——98 tf

William Ashley placed newspaper advertisements for 100 "enter-prising young men" to go to the headwaters of the Missouri River for one or more years to trap beaver and expand the fur trade. Je-didiah Smith and Jim Bridger were among the first group, known as "Ashley's Hundred," and became famous mountain men.

were mobbed with customers, vociferously objecting to inflated prices. Groups would relax in the shade swapping tales of the past year and renewing friendships. Eschewing codes of civilized conduct was condoned. Nefarious activities, fueled by alcohol, considered unacceptable in civilized society, were the norm: gambling, horse racing, shooting contests, fights, scalp dances, and comely Indian maidens luring men into the cottonwoods in exchange for a few trinkets. It was boisterous, disorderly mayhem. Then there were everyday chores: watering horses, rotating pastures, tanning robes, cooking, making lodges, mending clothes, and putting up pemmican. These wildly extravagant vacations lasted two or three weeks. Flush with new gear and fresh, clean clothes, individuals or groups drifted off to some promising valley to begin the fall trapping season. These raucous gatherings of Indians, mountain men, and traders became the hallmark of the mountain man epoch.

With pack trains and keelboats, the transportation needs of the fur trade were met for nearly two decades, but the enormous profits to be made by extracting ever larger quantities of fur and robes demanded an ever more efficient transportation system. The steamboat era was about to begin.

CHAPTER 9

Early Steamers

IN THEIR WILDEST IMAGINATIONS, Lewis and Clark, wranglers of Ashley's pack trains, and keelboaters could not conceive that blocky, steam-powered behemoths three-stories high would be transporting tons of goods and thousands of passengers up the Missouri. Collapsing banks, unpredictable currents, sandbars, and submerged and floating logs guarded the upper reaches of the river. Keelboat men testified about the deadly nature of the river, and navigation by steamboats was ascertained to be impossible. However, bankers and investors foresaw enormous profits, and they commissioned carpenters, iron workers, and engineers to design and build steamboats to tackle the Big Muddy and prove the impossible, possible.

In 1801, Robert Fulton, an American living in Paris, turned his inquisitive mind to nautical engineering and the potential of steam-powered ships. Fulton constructed a modest ship and launched the novelty on the Seine, where it attracted a crowd of doubters. Initially a success, the hull split and the invention sank.

Undaunted, a wiser Fulton returned to New York and engaged competent shipwrights and metal workers to build a steamer to his specifications. The vessel, powered by a wood-fired, steam-belching boiler, its design much improved over the French model, measured 146 feet long and 12 feet wide. A crude, piston-driven engine drove a pair of side-mounted paddlewheels.

In August 1807, risking reputation and investor money, Fulton declared his boat ready to power its way 150 miles up the Hudson River to Albany. To the awe of an expectant, but skeptical crowd, the vessel belched black smoke and clanked up the river at the astounding speed of 5 miles per hour. A day and a half later the steamer docked at Albany, completing a journey that took nearly a week using sail power. People that had labeled the vessel "Fulton's Folly" cheered and waved handkerchiefs, having witnessed the harnessing of steam power. Fulton's well-constructed boat and reliable engine doomed the "Age of Sail" and paved the way for unimagined commerce on the Mississippi, Ohio, and Missouri rivers.

In May 1811, five years after the Corps of Discovery's return to St. Louis, the first steamboats regularly challenged the lower Missouri. These prototype crafts were underpowered side-wheelers restricted to the deeper, less perfidious water. The engines were large and heavy, and, because they stood vertically, the piston action incessantly pounded on the framework of the hull. These early boats transported freight and passengers a few miles upriver from St. Louis. Elaborately carved figureheads distinguished each steamboat, and some early vessels were fitted with masts and sails. They had a six-foot draft and were subject to mechanical breakdowns.

After 1815, higher pressure engines increased speeds, boat sizes, and cargo capacities. In 1819, the little side-wheeler *Independence*, a slightly improved craft, left St. Louis and traveled 250 miles upstream to the tiny village of Chariton. It carried a cargo of flour, sugar, whiskey, and iron castings. It was lauded as a one-time miraculous achievement but by

1829 steamboats were making routine tips from St. Louis to Fort Leavenworth, Kansas.

Over a period of 80 years, the structural designs of steamboats and their power source remained fundamentally unchanged. Some modifications were made in hull designs, engines, and superstructures, considering where and how the boats would be used. Transporting passengers and cargo to the Upper Missouri and Fort Benton presented unique problems versus plying the deeper, less obstructed waters of the Ohio or Mississippi rivers. Over time, improved engineering contributed to more sumptuous, dependable steamers. A Mr. Edwards, clerk on the steamer *Henry M. Shreve*, left the levee at St. Louis in 1869 and recorded his thoughts, "Fifty years had passed since *Independence's* first incursion on the Big Muddy and paddle-wheel vessels had not only proliferated on its waters but, having gone through a long process of evolution in Ohio River builders' yards, had finally become reasonably dependable instruments of transportation. Still shoals, rapids, snags—and greed continued to bring them to grief."

Before 1830, the holds of river steamers averaged about eight feet in depth, but later, newly designed rectangular frames and increased lengths and widths of the vessels decreased hull depths. These and other ongoing design changes made it possible for steamers to challenge the Upper Missouri's sandbars and rapids.

CHAPTER 10

Upper Missouri Steamboats Come of Age

COMMISSIONED BY THE AMERICAN FUR COMPANY, the Louisville-built steamer *Yellowstone* reached Fort Union, three miles above the Yellowstone River's confluence with the Missouri, 2,000 miles above St. Louis, in 1833. Trips were then regularly made between St. Louis and Fort Union, eliminating a substantial portion of overland travel to the Rocky Mountains and providing a more expedient and profitable means of transporting furs to the east.

After the *Yellowstone* reached Fort Union in 1833, 26 years would pass before the first steam-powered craft would reach Fort Benton, Montana, the terminus of navigable water. Increasingly shallow water and the "Great Falls" of the Missouri prevented steamboats from penetrating further upstream. (It took the Lewis and Clark Expedition 18 days to portage canoes and baggage around the multiple waterfalls).

Early experimental steamboats had spawned fleets of shallow-draft (31 inches), wider-beamed vessels: multi-tiered, smoke-spewing, water-thrashing, 100- to 200-foot-long leviathans capable of transporting 300- to 400-tons of freight and 200 passengers 2,300 miles from St. Louis to Fort Benton. But not until 1859 did the 165-foot-long steamer *Chippewa*, captained by John LaBarge, attempt to reach Fort Benton. In command of a 95-man crew, he attempted the unattainable, to travel 650 miles from Fort Union at the mouth of the Yellowstone River up the Missouri to Fort Benton. He ran aground 12.5 miles short of his goal but concluded that with suitable boats and careful navigation, the trip from St. Louis to Fort Benton could be completed in 35 days. (LaBarge was overly optimistic. Voyages averaged 60 to 65 days.) The next year, on July 2, 1860, the *Chippewa* and *Key West* reached Fort Benton, saluted by the roar of gunfire and a raucous crowd. The infant town had gained an artery to the outside world that would bring them amenities from civilization.

The Upper Missouri had momentarily submitted to the power of steam, a contest that would ebb and flow for decades, each side gaining or losing depending on a multiplicity of factors: pilot skill, steamer construction, the strength, timing and volume of spring runoff, tonnage of freight, and the annual rearrangement of the Missouri's channel by the corrosive action of the current.

In the mid-nineteenth century there were no professional marine architects designing steamboats, but as the following description illustrates, the schemes of vessels were well thought out and practical, utilizing limited space to full advantage. Ronald R. Switzer in his book *The Steamboat Bertrand* relates the comments of a passenger in 1867 who was traveling on the steamer *Deer Lodge*, who had an eye for detail: "The general construction is simple. The hull is flat, almost without a keel, made to displace as little water as possible. When completely loaded, it does not draw more than 4 feet of water, averaging 3 to 3 ½ ft. Under the first deck, the hull forms the hold where the merchandise is stacked one half to two thirds of the length of the boat, the forward deck

The 165-foot-long Chippewa, *shown here, was the first steamboat to reach Fort Benton, Montana, the most distant port on the Missouri River. She and the* Key West *arrived on July 2, 1860, after leaving St. Louis on May 3. The regular arrival of steam-powered mechanical vessels rapidly altered the centuries-old cultures and economies of the Upper Missouri. The* Key West *operated for several years, but the very next year the* Chippewa *caught fire and exploded near the mouth of the Poplar River. The fire started from a lit candle when a crew member secretly tried to siphon whiskey from a barrel in the dark cargo hold. Fearing an imminent explosion when the fire reached the boat's 237 kegs of gunpowder, the crew and passengers abandoned ship. The* Chippewa *drifted downstream two miles before a massive explosion blew it to bits.* STATE HISTORICAL SOCIETY OF NORTH DAKOTA.

is open. The stern is closed in a room to protect the engines and serves as a repair shop. The furnaces and boilers are on the deck, forward of the engines. They pile firewood port, starboard, and forward, leaving a passage for the crew on each side of it. In front of the furnaces, there is an open stairway which leads up to the Upper Deck. This deck supported the length of the boat by cast iron columns, encloses a dining room or salon in the center, from which all cabins open on port and starboard. Outside the cabins on both sides there is a gallery onto which each cabin opens by a glass door. The great paddle board wheel which propels her is as wide as the stern. The pilot house, which contains the wheel is located on the upper deck between two high smokestacks and a little astern. She was armed with a field piece and carried both a carpenter and a black smith." (*The Steamboat Bertrand*)

By the early 1860s, long, horizontal boilers driving paired cylinders became standard for the period. Reduction in the height and number of decks, especially on the upper-river craft, decreased wind resistance and lowered the centers of gravity, increasing a boat's maneuverability. Advanced technologies repositioned the side-mounted paddlewheel to the stern, providing more power and control when navigating shallow water, landing along a riverbank, or docking at makeshift wharves. Later the paddlewheels were moved from recesses in the stern to extend beyond the stern, making them less vulnerable to snags.

By the mid-1860s as many as seven steamboats a day might tie up at Fort Benton to disgorge cargo and passengers. Smoke stacks and boat hulls resembled a city unto itself. Including the Mississippi River from New Orleans, the newly prosperous settlement of Fort Benton was, and is, the world's innermost port.

Before steamboats, the overland journey to the foot of the

The independently owned Deer Lodge *was built in 1865 at Belle Vernon, Pennsylvania, for the Upper Missouri trade. The very next year she made a profit of $45,000 (about $660,000 in value today) on one run to Fort Benton. Unique among the Missouri river steamers, she carried a portable saw to cut wood for her boilers. The* Deer Lodge *was dismantled in 1874.* MURPHY LIBRARY SPECIAL COLLECTIONS, UNIVERSITY OF WISCONSIN-LA CROSSE.

Rocky Mountains took 3 to 5 months. Carrying 250 to 300 tons of freight and passengers, a steamboat could make the journey in 1 to 2 months, and return to St. Louis is less time, its hold filled with buffalo robes, furs, gold, and passengers either disgruntled with life on the frontier or wearing money belts filled with gold dust.

Significant tonnages of cargo would be disgorged at points along the voyage. On July 14, 1867, 3,100 sacks of flour were unloaded at the mouth of the Musselshell River to be freighted overland to Fort Sims, Montana. On the evening of September 10, six double wagons, each pulled by six yoke of oxen, arrived from Browning, Montana, to load a recently docked cargo of flour, sugar, and coffee promised to the Indians. In 1868, 75 percent of the freight bound for the Northwest passed through Fort Benton. Between 1859 and 1890, 600 mountain boats docked at Fort Benton, carrying about 165,000 tons of freight of every imaginable description.

Steamboat construction averaged around $40,000. The value of freight ranged in the tens of thousands of dollars. Sometimes the profits on a single voyage were sufficient to repay the vessel's construction costs and the crew's wages. Freight rates from St. Louis to Fort Benton averaged eleven cents per pound. Cabin rates for passengers, one way from St. Louis to Fort Benton, was about $300, while deck passage was $75. Priority was always given to the more lucrative freight, which limited accommodations for passengers.

In the mid-1860s, various steamboat freight ledgers recorded, in one year, enormous profits for the time: *Deer Lodge*, $45,000; *Cora* $50,000, and in 1867 the *Peter Balen* logged freight receipts totaling a mind-boggling $80,000, more than $1 million in value today. Baring mishaps, the trip to Fort

Cargo from the Nellie Peck *has been off-loaded on the levee at Fort Benton. Barrels usually held salt pork, beef, gun powder, and whiskey; wooden boxes contained canned and bottled food, tobacco, medicines, and various household goods and business supplies; the burlap sacks likely had flour and grains, especially cornmeal. Other cargo included clothing, tools, mining supplies, wagon and stagecoach parts, building materials, and livestock.*

OVERHOLSER HISTORICAL RESEARCH CENTER, FORT BENTON.

Benton averaged 60 days. Few enterprises at the time could generate those large sums of money in such a short time.

Pushed hard and always subject to hazards, the service life of a river steamer plying the waters of the Upper Missouri was typically three years. This turnover accounted for about 400 different steamers operating on Montana's portion of the Missouri between 1860 and 1888.

The spark to build a fleet of technologically advanced steamboats kindled a fire in the hearts of men who could see the potential of limitless commerce. The discovery of gold-fields in Montana, the millions of buffalo robes yet to be harvested, and agricultural and ranching lands for the taking, proved the speculators correct. Steamboats were well patronized by a relentless tide of men and women traveling west to quell a restless spirit.

A steamboat is moored at Cow Island Landing, about 127 river miles below Fort Benton, in the summer of 1880. A small cluster of tents makes the temporary Cow Island "camp." In low water, especially in summer after spring runoff had subsided, steamboats couldn't pass the Dauphine Rapids above Cow Island, so cargo was offloaded here, where overland freight wagons took the cargo the rest of the way to Fort Benton. Cow Island was one of the few places where the rugged Missouri River Breaks opened up enough to allow wagons to reach the river. The wide expanse was an historic river crossing for native tribes. Montana Historical Society Research Center Photograph Archives, Helena, Montana.

CHAPTER 11

Ho! For the Gold Mines!

THE FIRST RECORDED GOLD STRIKE in Montana was made by James and Granville Stuart at Gold Creek in 1858, near present-day Drummond, Montana. The strike soon played out and the small settlement of American Fork fell into abandonment as the residents scrambled to the next rumored glory hole. Montana's first significant gold rush began in the summer of 1862. A profitable placer mine deposit discovered at Grasshopper Creek drew hundreds of gold-crazed miners, founding the town of Bannack City. In five months the settlement's population swelled to 500 persons, all needing supplies and mining equipment.

The discovery of gold in the Northern Rockies precipitated a gold rush, luring tens of thousands of prospectors, all confident of striking it rich. Gold, like a siren call, attracted bold, adventurous men of every race and creed. Some were virtuous while others were of lowly scruples. All were in an uninhibited scramble for wealth. Rascals, knowing easy profits could be had at the expense of miners starved for amenities and vice, followed the miners like hounds on a scent. Prostitutes, liquor peddlers, gamblers, swindlers, thieves, claim jumpers, and general hell raisers all wanted a piece of the action. This mass of humanity needed a means to reach the gold fields. Traveling overland from St. Louis was slow,

Another steamboat stop on the Upper Missouri in Montana was Coal Banks Landing, shown here in 1880. Named for a layer of coal in the area's hillsides, Coal Banks Landing was used frequently during the Indian Wars of 1876-1877. Today, located near Virgelle, Montana, Coal Banks Landing is the primary launch point for canoeists embarking on the Wild and Scenic Upper Missouri River through the Upper Missouri River Breaks National Monument. Montana Historical Society Research Center Photograph Archives, Helena, Montana.

tedious, and risked Indian attacks, not to mention the difficulties of reaching St. Louis from points east. The coincidental, successful navigation of the Missouri by steamboats all the way to Fort Benton and the discovery of gold were the catalysts that began an economic boom, and Fort Benton's quays became the fountainhead for the boom.

News of a big gold strike at Virginia City, Montana, in 1863 spread like a contagious virus in a crowded room. It took only 18 months for 10,000 miners to rush to Alder Gulch, birthing the boom towns of Virginia City and Nevada City. In less than a year Virginia City boasted a population of several thousand and was Montana's largest town. In five years, the placer mines and dredging operations around Alder Gulch produced $40 million of the yellow metal. Subsequent strikes in Montana included Silver Bow Creek near present-day Butte, and in July 1864, Last Chance Gulch, where the town of Helena is today. The diggings at Helena yielded $19 million of gold in the first four years. Diamond City came into existence because of a strike in Confederate Gulch east of Helena. Ten thousand miners extracted $19 million of gold there in four years.

In July 1864, an unprecedented number of mines with gold in profitable quantities were discovered at multiple locations: the Fraser River in British Columbia, in Washington Territory, and in Idaho. Demands on steamboats increased. In 1865 in St. Louis, the Montana and Idaho Transportation Line distributed hand bills titled "HO! FOR THE GOLD MINES!" The company offered overland passage via wagon train from Fort Benton to the gold fields of Virginia City, Bannack, Helena, Deer Lodge, and all points in outlying mining districts. Included in the hand bill were the departing dates for the steam ships: *Deer Lodge*, Saturday March 4;

The Baker Line placed this advertisement in The Helena Independent *newspaper in 1878, promoting "the elegant and commodious" steamboats* Red Cloud *and* Nellie Peck *arriving at Fort Benton around May 10. The advertisement claimed the boats would provide regular service between Fort Benton and Bismarck, North Dakota, during the "boating season" and offer "unprecedented facilities for comfort and despatch (sic)."*

The steamboat Josephine *is shown moored at the Fort Benton levee. This famous boat plied both the Upper Missouri and Yellowstone rivers, often under the command of Captain Grant Marsh. In 1874 Marsh piloted the* Josephine *to Fort Benton on three different trips, arriving on June 1, June 22, and July 22. Three trips in one season was a rare feat, and Marsh almost made it four. On his fourth attempt, low water forced Marsh and the* Josephine *to stop at Cow Island on August 28. No docks or wharves were ever built at Fort Benton; cargo and passengers crossed gangplanks.* Overholser Historical Research Center, Fort Benton.

Benton, Saturday, March 11; *Bertrand,* Thursday, March 16; and the *Yellowstone,* Saturday, March 18. The fee for overland transportation from Fort Benton to Helena, a distance of approximately 131 miles, was $25.

Between 1863 and 1869, 143 steamboats successfully arrived at Fort Benton, carrying people with interests in gold mining. From the spring of 1866 to the fall of 1877, some 70 steamboats carried 10,000 passengers into Montana. In the same period a single boat, the *Luella,* carried $1.25 million in gold dust down the Missouri, earning a $25,000 profit for the boat's owners. Included in the profits was a full complement of passengers paying $300 for cabin passage (probably not single occupancy). In time, Montana became a significant player in the amount of gold extracted from the earth in North America.

CHAPTER 12

Fort Benton, Montana, the World's Most Inland Port

As St. Louis was the location from which the thrust into the Northwest originated, so was Fort Benton the town from which all commercial activities were launched to specific regions of the Upper Missouri, Washington State, Idaho, and southwestern Canada. By 1866, Montana, with a population of 28,000, was second only to California in gold extraction. Ambitious merchants and freighters recognized opportunity, and Fort Benton (named for Missouri's Senator Thomas Hart Benton) became the hub of a web of wagon trails transporting miners, freight caravans, and an eclectic mix of opportunists, gamblers, prostitutes, shopkeepers, bankers, speculators, and saloon keepers to the gold fields. Everyone needed a stake: clothes, food, tools, machinery, draft animals, hardware, and housing. The values of commodities reaching Fort Benton were significantly marked up, securing huge profit margins for steamboat owners and captains and self-financed merchants seeking to double or triple their investments. There were three reasons for the exorbitant prices: the demand for supplies exceeded availability; the high costs of transporting goods up the Missouri; and once the supplies were off-loaded and stacked on the river bank, they were then repackaged by

Tons of off-loaded cargo weigh down the levee at Fort Benton in the 1870s. From 1860 to 1890, more than 600 steamboat landings were made at Fort Benton. During the peak between 1877 and 1883, more than 30 steamboats landed each year. Fifty-four landings, a record, occurred in 1878. Most boats arrived in May, June and early July. The volume and cost of the incoming freight was enormous, but the value of furs and gold taken downstream was even greater. In this photo, Colonel George Clendenin, the agent for the Coulson Line of steamboats, rests atop multiple barrels. A steamboat is moored farther down the levee. Overholser Historical Research Center, Fort Benton.

a transportation industry that moved the goods to the gold camps by mule or bull trains, wagons, or stage lines. "All trails lead out of Benton" was a familiar statement.

Several "bull trains" line up along Levee Street in Fort Benton in the 1870s. Pulled by upwards of 14 double-yoked oxen, the large freight wagons (often two or three wagons hitched together) transported goods from the steamboats to Helena and other gold camps. Freight from Fort Benton also made its way to Idaho and Washington over the Mullan Road. OVERHOLSER HISTORICAL RESEARCH CENTER, FORT BENTON.

Steamboats could only reach Fort Benton during two brief windows of time. The river levels rose twice a year, once in April, when spring rains and a warm sun melted the prairie snow, and a second time in May or June when the massive snowfields in the mountains were liquefied. It was only then that many, but not all, sandbars, rock-studded rapids, and logs would be submerged to a depth greater than the 36-inch draft of the steamboats. Each season, the amount and timing of water funneled into the Missouri's channel depended on weather conditions, varying by days or weeks.

Two overland routes also served the Montana mining camps: wagons trains from Salt Lake City, and pack trains from Portland. But overland transportation of goods, because of Indians closing the overland routes, highway men, inefficient use of time, tonnage limitations, inclement weather, and demands of draft animals, could not compete with the huge volumes of supplies being moved more efficiently by steamboats.

In 1860, the year the first steamboat reached Fort Benton, another marvelous engineering feat stimulated the development of Fort Benton, making it the undisputed center of commerce for the Northwest. In 1853 U.S. Army Captain John Mullan began surveying a military road from the Upper Missouri to Walla Walla, Washington. Mullan completed the project in 1860, overcoming impossible terrain and major river crossings, surmounting the Continental Divide near Helena, Montana. The Mullan Road linked the Upper Missouri drainage with the headwaters of the Columbia River. In a way, the road fulfilled President Jefferson's dream of a commercial water route through the Rockies. Indeed, merchandise and people could be moved from Europe to New Orleans or New York and on to Oregon or Washington Territories via North America's navigable waterways. The long, grievous journey around the tip of South America could be avoided.

Fort Benton became the port of departure for the Mullan Road on its way to Walla Walla, Helena, Alder Gulch, Bannack City, the Whoop-Up Trail which led into Canada, and the Fisk Wagon Road to St. Paul through northeast Montana and North Dakota. Other minor gold mining towns were served by branches off the Mullan Road.

Steamboat traffic to Fort Benton hit its stride in 1866. Thousands of miners unconcerned about physical inconveniences bought passages, averaging $150 per ticket, and space was limited. Miners, wrapped in blankets, slept on the decks, exposed to the elements and mosquitoes, and breathing incessant smoke vapors. They were the lucky ones. They could at least enjoy the scenery and cooling breezes. Others slept in squalor below decks on mattresses stuffed with rags, squeezed between boxes of freight, breathing grease and oil fumes. The lowliest crew men slept in hammocks hanging from hooks imbedded in the ship's timbers. Unremitting engine vibration and noise made sleep challenging. At least the ticket prices, because of competition, were less expensive.

A newspaper editorial appeared in *The New Northwest* describing Fort Benton: "In the street was a throng of varied and picturesque humanity; lumbermen from Minnesota and farmers from many parts of the great valley; Confederate sympathizers from Missouri and Union men from Western Reserve, miners from the Pacific coast , and fur traders and hunters of the vanishing northwestern wilderness; Indians of many tribes, desperadoes and lovers for order, miners, traders, clergymen, speculators, and land seekers, government officials, all the exuberant array of the American frontier."

Changes in mining techniques required different methods of handling and transporting heavier, more complex mining machinery. By the mid-1860s materials to build the huge dredges burrowing into the gravels of Alder Gulch came up river. By 1867 miners were burrowing deep into the earth to reach veins of gold locked in quartz deposits. The recovered ore had to be crushed in massive stamp mills. The effort to transport the weighty machinery from Ohio to the remote

The heavily laden Rose Bud *steams upriver near Downed Man's Rapids (aka Dead Men Rapids) about 85 miles below Fort Benton, below the confluence of Judith River. The* Rose Bud *was one of the few steamboats that made more than 50 trips to Fort Benton in her career. She was the first steamboat to reach Fort Benton in 1880, 1883, and 1886, and in 1887 she arrived on April 26, the earliest arrival in history. In 1882 the* Rose Bud *was equipped with electricity and became the first illuminated boat seen at Fort Benton.* Overholser Historical Research Center, Fort Benton.

Gravely Mountains was considerable, probably impossible were it not for steamboats.

By 1870 the gold rush had run its course. In 1871, Fort Benton's days as a jumping off point for men chasing the glitter of gold ebbed. The earth had yielded millions of dollars of the precious metal (at $15 dollars an ounce), but except for diehards working a few minor placer mines and panning remote streams, the party had ended.

Fort Benton's population plummeted from 500 full-time residents to 180 hearty souls. Only 8 steamboats reached Fort Benton that year. Businesses closed by the score: 14 saloons, 4 Indian trading posts, a brewery, a blacksmith shop, and a wagon construction and repair facility, to name a few. In the end, only a handful of determined individuals stayed on, hoping for new opportunities.

Immigrant families, taking advantage of staking out homesteads in Montana, Idaho, and Washington state, needed supplies, tools, stock, and wagons. Their numbers were swollen by settlers destined for the prairies of western Canada. Buffalo robes continued to be shipped to eastern cities until the early 1880s. Records show that between 1872 and 1882 buffalo hunters and Indians harvested 445,000 buffalo from the Northern Plains, their hides shipped by steamboat to St. Louis. The growth of merchandizing breathed new life into a staggered Fort Benton and caused a modest rebirth of steamboat traffic. By 1880 Fort Benton again had the look of a growing river city.

The encroaching railroads, offering a more productive, less costly means of moving freight, began to spread their tentacles into the Northern Plains, presenting a threat to the steamboat industry. Ignoring the ominous developments, 30 million pounds of freight were unloaded at Fort Benton's

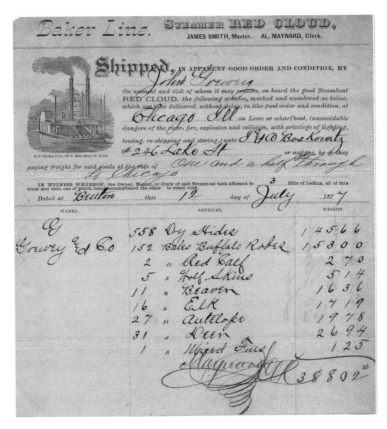

A shipping manifest for the Red Cloud *leaving Fort Benton on July 12, 1877, showed a cargo of hides and furs, mainly 558 buffalo hides and 152 bales of buffalo robes. Other furs included 16 elk, 27 antelope, 31 deer, and 11 beaver, a far cry from the thousands of beaver pelts sent east at the height of the beaver trade. The total weight of the hides and furs was 38,802 pounds, and the shipment was to be delivered to Chicago. The hides and furs were probably off-loaded at Sioux City or another downstream port and taken to Chicago by railroad.*

docks in the early 1880s. With growth came construction activities. In 1882 a brick kiln produced 3 million bricks to build residences and warehouses.

The Grand Union Hotel, the most luxurious in the northwest, occupied a prominent location on the bank of the Missouri in the heart of Fort Benton. Construction, financed locally, costing $30,000, began in 1881. In 15 months, brick masons fitted 500,000 bricks, raising the structure three stories. The construction costs exceeded budget by $20,000, and elaborate furnishings, most shipped upriver, commanded the princely sum of $150,000. The entire population of the town turned out for the grand opening, the event remembered as the most elaborate social occasion yet seen in Montana. The affair validated a new age of prosperity. A moribund Fort Benton had been reborn.

James J. Hill's St. Paul, Minnesota and Manitoba Railway (the Manitoba Road), the precursor to his Great Northern Railway, reached Fort Benton in 1887, negatively impacting the town's steamboat industry. Steam-powered behemoths, laboring up the Missouri for 60 days, transporting several tons of freight from St. Louis to Fort Benton, simply could not compete economically with steam-driven trains gliding on ribbons of steel. At St. Louis, west-bound freight shipped by steamer from the major east coast and mid-west commerce centers had to be repacked for the specially designed Missouri River steamers. Rail transport eliminated this expensive, cumbersome bottleneck. Freight shipped on rail cars from the commerce centers could stay on rail cars all the way to the expanding market places in the West. The era of the great river trade effectively ended in the early 1890s. A final private boat arrived in Fort Benton 1908, but it burned after striking the drawbridge at Fort Benton.

Fort Benton grew prosperous during the steamboat era. In 1882 the three-story Grand Union Hotel, built of bricks from a newly constructed kiln, opened to great fanfare. It was opulent for its time and place. In this photo, the steamboat O.K. *is moored beside the hotel.* OVERHOLSER HISTORICAL RESEARCH CENTER, FORT BENTON.

Despite changing economic fortunes, Fort Benton survived by adjusting to the developing livestock industry: cattle, sheep, and horses. Later, farmers immigrated west as a result of the Homestead Act of 1909. For several of years after the Homestead Act, unusually wet seasons generated extraordinary harvests of wheat and hay, and farmers prospered. Slowly, however, the Northern Plains showed the reality of the country. The normal seasons of sparse rainfall reappeared, causing a decade of drought. Grasshoppers and cut and wire worms wrecked crops. Over time, the prairie was pocked with abandoned homesteads moldering back into the earth. A few of the determined stuck it out. Some of the more brazen purchased additional acreages at fire-sale prices, embraced new

The 197-foot Benton *had a long and notable history on the Upper Missouri. She first arrived at Fort Benton on May 27, 1875, and made 44 trips to the port and 15 trips to other Montana points in her career. She is thought to have carried more freight to Fort Benton than any other boat. In late summer 1876 she was pressed into service by the U.S. Army to support soldiers trailing Sitting Bull and the Sioux after Custer's defeat at the Battle of the Little Bighorn, and the next year she served in the closing days of the Nez Perce War. Her last trip to Fort Benton was in 1887. She sank later that year after hitting a drawbridge at Sioux City. The* Benton *is also shown on the cover of this book.* St. Louis Mercantile Library at the University of Missouri-St. Louis cultivation techniques, and grew drought tolerant varieties of wheat. Descendants of the hardiest remain on the land today.

Today, Fort Benton is one of the permanent towns along the Missouri River, serving local agriculture and embracing tourism, including a growing number of river enthusiasts who enjoy paddling canoes down the still primitive 140-mile stretch of river between Fort Benton and James Kipp State Park.

CHAPTER 13

Steamboat Construction and Operation

To satisfy the insatiable demands for freight of every description, it is estimated that 700 different designs of steamboats tested the Missouri between 1819 and the end of the steamboat era in 1890. To shorten travel time, more powerful engines were designed, risking boiler explosions. To glide more easily over sandbars and shoals, hulls were made more flexible, risking fractured support beams. Deeper hulls could accommodate more freight but risked long and laborious delays warping and "grasshoppering" over sandbars and rapids. Engineers continually queried vessel pilots, soliciting ideas about how to construct the ideal river steamer.

Upper Missouri vessels had to be engineered differently than any that had come before. The result was an odd looking, flat-bottomed, many tiered, smoke-belching colossus that slid over the water rather than slice through it. Steamboats were wasteful of energy. Builders knew the boats' huge demands for fuel could be met by the forests along the river. Because monetary returns demanded speed, power, and performance, safety took a back seat. Pushing steam-generating boilers beyond their limits popped rivets and shredded cast iron, spewing scalding steam and fire. The typical Upper Missouri "mountain boat" was utilitarian, designed as a no-

In this photo the Helena *is tied up on the Missouri River near the mouth of the Marias River in 1878, during her first trip to Fort Benton. In her inaugural voyage, she took 235 tons of freight and 56 passengers to Fort Benton, arriving on May 14. In the next 10 years she made more than 50 trips to Montana. In 1884 she was the first steamboat of the season at Fort Benton, arriving on May 6, a week ahead of other boats.* MONTANA HISTORICAL SOCIETY RESEARCH CENTER PHOTOGRAPH ARCHIVES, HELENA, MONTANA frills working boat. They were smaller, more homely boats than the large, stately, passenger friendly steamboats that sailed the deeper, less serpentine Mississippi. In the end, the ever changing nature of the Upper Missouri never permitted the perfect steamboat design.

All engineering changes took advantage of previous design failings, many influenced by pilots and crews with firsthand experiences. Boat and engine builders were found in the trades: water-wheel makers, blacksmiths, carpenters, plumbers, boat builders, iron workers, and liquor distillers with knowledge of crude boiler manufacture. Mechanics and iron workers invented novel ways of working metals, and carpenters sketched blueprints for wooden frameworks that could withstand the stresses placed on them. To save weight, boat builders used pine or popular rather than stronger, heavier oak to build decks and bulkheads.

Much of the boat building was invented on the spot, the artisans flying by the "seat-of–their-pants." In 1839, an engineer experimented with an iron hull, but despite being somewhat resistant to punctures from snags, the unfamiliar design failed to be accepted by rivermen. The knowledge and expertise to construct acceptable metal-hulled vessels was decades in the future, blooming to fruition in the Civil War.

Brownsville, Pennsylvania, located on the shore of the Monongahela River, 1,200 miles from the Missouri River, was the center of steamboat construction into the 1870s because the heavy industry for engine construction was nearby in Pittsburgh. Parts peculiar to steamboat construction were fabricated in distant locations and hauled to the boatyards. Prodigious quantities of wood were delivered and fashioned into boats by skilled tradesmen. Several boats would be under various stages of construction at any given time.

The Red Cloud *was one of the largest and fastest steamboats on the Upper Missouri. In 1877 she successfully made three separate trips to Fort Benton. On one of those trips, she made the 550-mile journey from Bismarck to Fort Benton in 8 days and 17 hours. This was an all-time record. In 1879, the* Red Cloud *carried 215 Canadian Mounted Police, 170 passengers, and a large number of horses, mules, cattle, and sheep to Fort Benton in one trip. In 1882 she delivered 500 tons of freight to Fort Benton, but that July she was snagged and lost at Eight Point (later named Red Cloud Bend) above Fort Peck.* Murphy Library Special Collections, University of Wisconsin-La Crosse.

To facilitate carrying 200-plus tons of freight and 100 or more passengers over 36 inches of water, steamers took novel, never-before-seen shapes. The bow took on a slightly upturned spoon shape to facilitate sliding over sandbars, and the specially designed and positioned paddlewheel could operate in a scant six to eight inches of water. A wide, flat-bottomed hull with minimal freeboard permitted passage in only 20 inches of water when unloaded.

Steamboat performance was accomplished by stacking 80 percent of the superstructure in layered tiers. The high superstructure provided for the upward distribution of freight and passengers, eliminating the need for a deep-water craft. Immediately atop a steamer's broad hull stood the open-sided main deck; above the main deck stood the boiler deck; above the boiler deck stood a smaller deck that housed the officers; and perched on top was the wheel-house, walled on four sides by large windows, offering a 360-degree view of river hazards.

The forward section of the main deck housed the fire box, boilers, and firewood. Aft rested two piston engines, the throttle, and the steam escape pipes. A pipe, suspended from the ceiling, carried scalding hot steam from the boiler to the engine. A horseshoe-shaped expansion loop prevented rupturing of this critical component of the drive line.

The environment on the main deck was taxing: constant vibration, the unbearable heat in the area of the boiler, the noise of hissing steam, men swearing about the insatiable demands of the boilers for wood, and the clanking of the engine parts. The deck space between the boilers and engines held cargo and low-paying passengers. The complaints of the third-class passengers added to the cacophony.

The boiler deck above the main deck lodged the well-heeled passengers. The tiny, enclosed compartments were

Spartan, often sleeping multiple passengers. At the bow of the boat, in front of the smoke stacks, was the hurricane deck, an extension of the boiler deck. This popular, open-railed deck offered bracing weather and expansive views of unspoiled wilderness, changing with each bend of the river. However, open decks also offered a more nefarious activity, one that would be considered odious in contemporary society.

All boats had, on top, a box-shaped wheelhouse located aft of, and between, the paired smoke stacks. This small structure provided the primary means of safely navigating the mercurial nature of the Missouri. A massive steering wheel was connected by linkages to four spaced, triangle-shaped rudders mounted in front of the paddle wheel. A skilled pilot, by rotating the steering wheel, adjusting the angle of the rudders at just the precise moment, could maneuver the ponderous craft around snags and shifting sand bars, through shoals and rapids, and angle his boat into hurricane-force prairie winds. Inattentive or slow-to-anticipate pilots commonly met with disaster.

Wheelhouses were stenciled with the boat's name in bold letters, and often carved around the perimeter were ornate, personalized, wooden ornamentation. Mounted on the wheelhouse, busts of bull elk, running deer, or sunbursts were fashionable. Some pilots took the precaution of wrapping the wheelhouse in bulletproof sheet metal for protection against sniping Indians.

The thrust to overcome a current swollen by heavy spring snowmelt that could reach a speed of 10 miles per hour was provided by a paddlewheel, a wooded cylinder fitted with horizontal wood paddles and belted with cast iron. The stern paddlewheel varied in size depending on a boat's length and weight, but averaged about 18 feet in diameter and 24 feet wide. Two piston-driven engines, located in the stern on either side of the hull, were connected by piston rods to the paddlewheel cranks, which rotated the wheel about 20 times per minute. When the nature of the river demanded faster rotations, the danger of a catastrophic boiler explosion loomed. The trick was to gorge the firebox with enough wood to generate sufficient power, but not so much as to rupture the boilers, blowing the ship into splinters.

After 1850 steam-powered whistles came in vogue. To have maximum range, they were mounted high on the boats in the vicinity of the wheelhouses. The inherent unpredictability of river conditions made arrivals at ports-of-call highly inconsistent. One can only imagine the stir created—among both passengers and settlement residents—when a boat's whistle echoed around a bend in the river, signaling its approach. After tying up to the bank or dock, passengers could wander about the communities, getting a feel for life on the frontier. Residents would board the boat to query the nature of the boat's manifest and make purchases.

Because fast boats piloted by daring captains won freight contracts, the ponderous, unwieldy steamboats, not uncommonly, engaged in races. Boats competed, particularly early in the spring, to be the first to deliver freight to customers. Due to boat sizes and the limitations of steam power, the contests were brief, frequently ending at a bend or a sandbar. Not uncommonly, an impassioned pilot, stationed in the wheelhouse, could not bear to find himself looking at another boat's stern. Upon rounding a bend and sighting another boat, the pilot would call for "more steam." A boisterous—bordering on rowdy—exchange of whistles, shouts, and gunfire erupted when one boat passed another. Had the vessels not been separated by a few feet of water, fisticuffs surely would have erupted.

On June 6, 1862, Samuel Houser, a young man convinced

of finding his fortune in Montana's gold diggings, experienced a duel between the competing steamboats *Emilie* and *Spread Eagle*. In route to Fort Benton, the vessels launched from their overnight moorings at Fort Berthold, North Dakota. The *Spread Eagle* had departed St. Louis four days ahead of *Emilie*, but with straining boilers and rattling engines, the *Emilie* closed the gap. Challenges were shouted and the race to reach Fort Benton commenced. Hauser, aboard the *Emilie*, recounts the story: "Our boat waited until the other shoved off. Gathering steam to the last notch, we followed, the boat trembling like a fig leaf at each puff. Accumulated steam soon carried us past them and such a shouting you've never heard." The cheers on *Emilie*'s decks settled into subdued disbelief as the *Spread Eagle* generated sufficient steam to re-take the lead. "All turned imploringly to the pilot. He talked through the pipes to the engineer, and in a few minutes the distance between us was diminishing and faces began to brighten." For at least an hour the two boats were in a dead heat. Boilers pushed to rupturing, neither could get an advantage. Ahead appeared an island submerged by spring runoff but not deep enough to navigate over. *Spread Eagle* turned toward the deeper but more circuitous main channel. Opposite the submerged island appeared a narrow chute of swift water of unknown depth, offering a shortcut. The *Emilie*'s pilot, who also owned the boat, rolled the dice.

Not yet uncommitted to the main channel, the pilot of the *Spread Eagle* suddenly recognized the shorter channel was navigable. Loath to fall behind, he abruptly changed course and rammed, bow first, into the *Emilie*. Although the impact nearly struck *Emilie*'s boilers, which would have destroyed both vessels in a horrendous explosion, she was not disabled. However, the two boats became fastened together, drifting out-of-control downriver as if locked in a death spiral. A wild uproar consumed both boats. Face to face, crews, officers, and passengers threatened one another to the point of gunfire. Unable to be steered, the conjoined boats drifted for some time like a wounded duck. "Fortunately," Hauser related, "the two boats separated of their own accord and our engineer, without orders, turned on the last pound of steam causing us to glide by." *Emilie* reached Fort Benton eleven days later, four days ahead of the *Spread Eagle*. The saloons were rife with bragging and embellishments about how the *Emilie* "whipped" the *Spread Eagle*.

The pulsating hearts of a steamboat were multiple wood-fired boilers, and like mammalian hearts pulsing blood through arteries, the boilers fed hot steam into pipes leading to huge piston engines. Constructed of wrought iron and cylindrical in shape, as many as three boilers were mounted parallel, most often in the bow. The gaping mouth of the fire box opened toward the bow so downstream wind would act as a bellows. Exiting the fire box were paired chimneys or funnels, rising through the vessel to a height of nearly 100 feet above the upper deck. The chimneys were stabilized by lacing together a series of cables, the stacks appearing like the extended antennae of a giant beetle.

A series of boilers resting on an unstable platform had a serious intrinsic fault. Structurally, the boat's boilers were connected by pipes designed to maintain equal water levels in each boiler. Unequal distribution of freight or running aground on a sandbar could make the boat list, tilting the boilers and causing the highest boiler to drain. The red-hot metal, suddenly deprived of water, would fail, likely rupturing the adjacent boilers and at best releasing a roaring hot column of steam or at worst causing an explosion.

Feeding the boilers with just the right amount of wood to maintain an optimum boil required considerable skill and experience, tempered with instinct. Too little fuel reduced speed, too much increased boiler pressure. The technical details about how quickly steam pressure rose were an enigma to the best minds of the day. This continued to be an inexact science until the mid-1850s, when reasonably reliable steam and water pressure gages came into use. The new instruments warned when boilers were running dry or stream pressures were becoming dangerous. Boilers after 1860 produced enormous amounts of power, but, on several occasions, boilers pushed beyond their structural integrity by pilots demanding more speed proved fatal to steamer and passengers.

Water, dipped from the river, fed the boilers, but the composition of the water caused considerable aggravation. The copious amounts of silt and sand in the Missouri proved to be the Achilles' heel of a boiler, and dealing with the residual sediment after a day's travel remained an inherent, obstreperous problem. At the end of a day's run, the boiler fires were extinguished and the boilers opened and drained. A lowly crew man crawled into a boiler's confined space and tediously shoveled out the steaming muck. Eventually, a method was found to blow out the debris while the boat was under way, but like an insidious, uncontainable demon bent on destruction, abrasive silt and sand slithered aft through pipes into the engines, abrading the pistons and valves. This contributed to the short three- or four-year working life of a steamboat operating on the Upper Missouri.

The inherent difficulties with boilers were compounded by feckless "boiler engineers" of inferior intellect. Pilots of high character hired reliable, experienced engineers, while others overlooked drunkenness or sloth, putting passengers, boats, and freight at risk. Boiler engineers earned salaries from the boat owners of about $200 per month (a very good wage for the time), a little more if his skills included working with wrought iron. Equipment failures were common and a stalled vessel 1,500 miles up the Missouri could expect no help.

In 1838, to overcome slipshod construction and mechanical failures, particularly deadly boiler explosions, Congress passed a law requiring federal inspection of steamboats, resulting in a gradual reduction in mechanical failures and increased passenger safety. The law meshed nicely with increasing boiler pressures and the indignation expressed by passengers concerned about safety and foolhardy pilots. But no law reached into the engine room when engineers, faced with a stretch of fast water or the need to surmount a rapid, closed safety valves to build a "wad of steam" for a burst of power. It was not uncommon for animated exchanges to take place between a steamer's pilot demanding "more steam" and the sound judgment of a competent, experienced engineer.

When facing difficult water, a pilot would call through the "speaking tube" to the engineer, demanding more steam, hoping for the best. The engineers and pilots relied on their ears and the deck vibrations to gage power and the strain on boilers. The high pressure, single-cylinder steam engines exhausted steam with predictable thunder-like sounds that could be heard for miles upriver. As boiler pressure increased the racket would increase in volume and frequency. Getting maximum steam without overtaxing the boilers demanded a delicate balancing act.

The deeper and less obstructed lower Missouri, Mississippi, and Ohio Rivers saw the use of double-engine side-wheelers. By careful application of unequal power to the paddlewheel, the boat could be maneuvered into the

The William J. Lewis *of the Missouri River Packet Company was one of the few side-wheel steamboats on the Upper Missouri. On her first trip, she departed St. Louis on March 27, 1866, docked at Fort Benton, and returned to St. Louis on June 17, earning the company a $60,000 profit (almost $1 million in value today) on the 4,600-mile round trip. The captain of that trip was paid $800 per month (about $12,000 in value today). One year the boat made two round trips from St. Louis to Fort Benton. Launched in 1866, she wrecked in 1873, her 7-year career about twice the average duration for an Upper Missouri steamboat.* MONTANA HISTORICAL SOCIETY RESEARCH CENTER PHOTOGRAPH ARCHIVES, HELENA, MONTANA.

crowded wharves of the major cities along the Ohio River and its tributaries. But side-wheelers had characteristics that made them unacceptable for the Upper Missouri: they were heavy, the side-mounted paddles were vulnerable to snags, and hulls were narrow, limiting cargo capacities. Because both engines ran at all times, the side-wheelers required two skilled engineers operating in synchronization to avoid sandbars and snags. Because of these limitations, mountain steamers were stern-wheelers. Their shallow draft increased freight tonnage, while still able to surmount sandbars and rapids. One unique advantage of stern-wheel power contributed greatly to successful navigation of the Upper Missouri. When grounded on a sandbar, the paddlewheel could be run in reverse, pushing water under the hull and raising the water level under the vessel. Often, the slightly increased buoyancy enabled the steamer to surmount a rapid or sandbar, avoiding the delay and labor of "grasshoppering" or warping the boat over an obstacle.

Boat owners and pilots, to increase freight tonnage and passenger numbers, demanded boats with ever shallower drafts, which reduced internal bracing of the hull. The tradeoff created problems. Hulls became so flexible that rounding an acute bend or humping over sandbars threw engines off their mounts and stressed steam pipes. Steam hissing from leaks would cook skin in seconds.

Shallow water caused problems maintaining power and speed. The laboring paddlewheel could not efficiently pull water through the narrow gap between the river bottom and hull. This caused the wheel to slow to as few as 14 revolutions a minute.

Many times every day the pilots and crews had to adjust to the idiosyncrasies of their state-of-the-art steam-powered vessels. Cool thinking and quick actions could rescue boats, crews, freight, and passengers when things went wrong. The vulnerability most feared and never fully conquered was fire. Even a steamer tied to a levee risked immolation. In 1869, a catastrophic fire occurred at a St. Louis levee. Fire, jumping from boat to boat, destroyed 7 steamers loaded with freight destined for Fort Benton. The cause of the inferno was never ascertained for certain.

CHAPTER 14

Wood Hawks: Crucial Suppliers

WOOD PROVIDED THE ENERGY to power a steamboat, and it was burned in prodigious quantities. A steamer typically burned 30 cords a day, or about 40 trees. The need created a new job description: wood hawk. Entrepreneurial wood hawks were the linchpin of the steamboat age. Without their services, steamboat traffic would not have existed, and the opening of the Northwest would have been delayed for decades.

Because steamboats slowed or stopped at the foot of rapids to gage the current's strength and water's depth, resourceful men set up primitive wood-cutting camps in proximity to the rapids. Frequently, more wood had to be taken onboard to get up enough steam to pass the rapids. At the infamous Dauphin Rapids upriver from Bismarck, North Dakota, wood hawking became a major industry. It was here, in August 1868, Indians attacked a wood-cutters camp, slaughtering seven men. The crew of the *Bertha*, needing wood, found the scalped bodies at the wood hawks' dug-out, some men in their bunks and others scattered about. They were buried in shallow graves stacked with stones to prevent being dug up by wolves.

Wood cutters led a primitive existence. Living quarters were dirty and primitive: small, drafty log shanties or stacked blocks of stone set into the earth. The dirt-floored structures were musty, damp, and leaked cold air. Their existence was enveloped by isolation, serious harassment by Indians, and exhausting labor. Since the tribes quickly learned that the wood camps were sources of liquor, food, guns, and ammunition, they were prime targets for raids. The more industrious and hardy wood cutters worked through the sub-zero winters to stockpile enough cords of wood to last through the spring and summer seasons. The cut timber was dragged by hand or horses to the river's edge, then cut to appropriate lengths and stacked. The logs were cut to lengths with a large cross-cut saw operated by two men.

Cutting and stacking 20 or more cords of wood demanded weeks of backbreaking labor. (A cord was a stack or wood about 4-feet high, 4-feet wide, and 8-feet long.) Food quality was poor and supplies were meager. Hard tack, beans, bacon, and fat pork provided sustenance, sometimes supplemented by venison, elk, or buffalo. Rather than being paid fully in cash, wood hawks would often trade wood for a more nutritious and varied diet: dried or canned fruits (currents, strawberries, or peaches), vegetables (tomatoes), coffee, salt and pepper, flour, and liquor. Steamer pilots, anxious to preserve cash, preferred to barter supplies for wood. The arrangement satisfied both parties. And, when ahead of schedule and an opportunity presented itself, pilots avoided purchasing wood by setting roustabouts ashore to cut wood. Huge piles of driftwood grounded at the point of an island, the logs meshed together like a giant pile of tossed tooth picks, presented a convenient opportunity to save money and labor.

Wood meant power. Keeping the lower deck piled with wood, either by purchasing from wood hawks or putting a crew ashore to scrounge drift wood, was usually delegated to a responsible individual. "Wood chief" was the most important title assigned to a crew member, and securing an adequate supply was the steamer's most continual and irksome problem. Haggling for fuel with men at the bottom of the socioeconomic ladder (wood hawks) required adroit communication talents. Wood hawks charged from $2.50 to an exorbitant $15 per cord, the price fluctuated depending on the desperation of the pilot. The log of one steamer recorded that in making the 67-day trip from St. Louis to Fort Benton, 1,051 cords of wood were burned at a cost of $6,048.70. The steamer stopped 71 times to take on wood. On average about $100 dollars per day was spent for fuel. The peak of steamer traffic occurred in 1867 when 39 boats destined for Fort Benton were using an average of 30 cords of wood per day.

Commerce always superseded any consideration for the deforestation of river bottom cottonwood and ash groves. Once the stands of accessible cottonwood trees were exhausted, the wood hawks attacked stands of pines cloaking the hills above the river. The heavy, awkward logs were dragged ever increasing distances by horses or manual labor. Dragging logs through coulees and over the undulating terrain required near superhuman effort.

Because the dry environment along much of the Upper Missouri in Montana is better suited for prairies than forests, finding wood to steam the final distance onto Fort Benton became problematic. Wood hawks were absent. A boat's crew would be put ashore to gather driftwood or cut down any sized living trees that could be found, causing delays of several hours or a day. Green cottonwood had to be coaxed into burning by dousing it in kerosene or slathering it with animal fat. As a last resort, wrecked steamers, whose skeletal remains were above water, were cannibalized for fuel.

The diary of young Peter Koch, who cut wood at the mouth of the Musselshell River in Montana in 1869 and 1870, describes in abbreviated phrases the misery and discouragement that was the tenuous life of a wood cutter on the Northern Plains. He is a sterling example of the resolute courage, fortitude, and mental toughness necessary to survive on the remote Missouri shore:

> Oct. 4. Commenced chopping. Blistered my hands and broke an axe handle.
>
> 8. Twenty five years old and poor as a rat. Cut down a tree on the cabin.
>
> 20. Cutting while Joe is on guard. Snow tonight.
>
> 24. Killed my first buffalo. He took 7 spencer and 6 pistol balls before he died. River full of Ice.
>
> Nov. 7. A gale of wind. Those Arapahoes who camped abt. 10 days at Jim Wells woodyard have moved down the river after shooting into his stockade.
>
> 15. Chopped hard all day. B. M. says 3 cords. Fred came back all wet. He had started in a skiff with Dick Harris, both got drunk, and upset on Squaw Creek.
>
> 25. Fred and Olsen started out wolfing. We stopped chopping on account of shooting and shouting in the hills. Joe and I found 4 wolves at our baits.
>
> Dec. 10 Sick. No meat.

11. Sick yet. Bill, Joe and Mills went to Musselshell, said the Indians had attacked and stolen 3 horses and a mule but lost one man.

24. Christmas eve. No wolves.

Jan. 16. Awful cold. Froze my ears.

17. Too cold to work. Went up to Musselshell. Froze my nose.

24. Thawing heavily. Mills drunk.

Mar. 22. Saw three geese. (Spring has come, gentle Annie.) Martin sick.

Apr. 24. Sixty Crows went up the river after Sioux to avenge the killing of 29 Crows. They were all looking dreadful, had their hair cut off, their fingers and faces cut, with the blood left on their faces.

May 9. One hundred and seventy cords on the bank. We put fire to the brush piles. The fire spread and burnt up 50 cords. We were played out before we got it checked. Nothing to eat.

13. Wind turned and started the fire again. About 20 cords burned.

22. The 'Nick Wall' passed about two o'clock in the morning without stopping.

23. 40-50 Indians showed themselves at Musselshell the 20th. The crazy Frenchman started toward them and was badly beaten but when firing stared they turned and ran.

24. Raining. The 'Ida Reese' passed about daybreak without our knowing it.

28. Sold 'Deerlodge' about 10 cords of wood.

June 13. The 'Sallie' passed after midnight and took 15 cords of wood.

16. The 'Ida Stockdale' passé without stopping. We threw 6 cords back from the bank to keep it from falling into the river.

July 4. Indians firing at us from nearest cottonwood trees and all through the sagebrush. The balls whistled pretty lively but we returned fire and drove them from their shelter. We went out and found one young warrior killed by a shot through the upper thigh. We got his gun, bow and arrows and two butcher knives and threw his body into the river. Waring scalped him.

Peter Koch and his fellows sold no more wood, and he gave up in the fall, heading southwest. He learned the surveying trade and, curiously, eventually directed Bozeman's First National Bank. Koch was an exception. Many nameless vagabonds labored as wood hawks and vanished into obscurity.

CHAPTER 15

Reading Water: Steamboat Navigation

THE AMOUNT OF WATER in the Missouri was crucial to successful navigation. To push their enormous bulk against the current, across sandbars, and over rapids, powered by relatively primitive engines, it was necessary to devise techniques—never before tried—to move freight and passengers to ports of call. Competent pilots memorized the locations of endless sandbars, rapids, bends, and rocks. Traveling unencumbered any distance on the Missouri was a pleasure seldom realized. Delays of hours or days caused aggravations to crews, passengers, and pilots, even though multiple methods to surmount a rough patch might be used to cope with the volatile nature of the river.

An ingenious design of cables, pulleys, and masts was rigged in the bow of each Upper Missouri steamer. When confronted with an impassible rapid or sandbar, two telephone-pole-sized spars were lowered to the bottom of the river ahead of the boat at a 45 degree angle. The configuration mimicked the arrangement of the rear legs of a grasshopper. Cables were attached from the bottoms of the spars to a rotating capstan (winch) powered by the steam engine. Slowly reeling in the cables, the vessel was walked or "grasshoppered" forward by brute force until the advance of the

The steamboats (from left) Far West, Nellie Peck, Western, Benton, *and an unnamed boat (far right) are loaded at the Bismarck levee in 1877 in preparation for the run to Fort Benton. Because the Upper Missouri River changed every year—carving new channels, reforming sandbars, and carrying different volumes of water—steamboat pilots had to "read" the river anew every trip, always looking for new hazards and better, faster, safer routes.* MONTANA HISTORICAL SOCIETY RESEARCH CENTER PHOTOGRAPH ARCHIVES, HELENA, MONTANA.

boat negated the leverage of the spars. The process was repeated yard by yard, sliding the boat forward until the steamer cleared the obstruction.

If sparing at first failed, the cargo would be shifted from the bow to the stern, and as a last resort a portion of the cargo and passengers would be put ashore to increase buoyancy. The process was inconvenient to the passengers and time consuming.

In years of extreme low water, boats advanced by the process of "double tripping." A portion of the cargo and sometime passengers were put ashore. Once the obstruction had been cleared, the passengers reboarded and the steamer proceeded to its destination, later returning for the cargo left at the rapids. Double tripping wasted time, increased fuel consumption, added wear and tear on the engines and boilers, and increased operating expenses. In 1869, the Missouri dropped to record low flows. Eighteen of 24 steamers bound for Fort Benton had to double trip from Dauphin Rapids.

In years of high water, the power of some rapids was too much for even the most powerful steamers or skilled pilots. In these instances, a "dead man" answered the need. With adroitness fraught with danger, trusted roustabouts wrestled a thick, long rope ashore, advanced upstream, and fastened it to a large, well planted tree or buried log. The boat's capstan slowly reeled in the rope, warping (winching) the steamer ahead inch by inch. The rope was then advanced to the next dead man, and the next, until the steamer cleared the rapid. If the rope snapped or the "dead man" tore out of the ground, the steamer would be whisked backwards or turned sideways, crashing into the rocks. Pilots, passengers, and crews resigned themselves to unrelenting days of sparring and dead-man winching.

For more than fifty years, Dauphin Rapids, roughly 125

miles downstream from Fort Benton, was the bane of steam-boat travel on the Upper Missouri, the worst of hundreds of navigation barriers obstructing the infamous river. Louis Dauphin had gained a degree of notoriety among steamboat captains during the height of steamboat traffic on the Big Muddy. He traded in meat, ranging the country between the big bends of the Missouri. He was well known for his woods savvy and hunting skills and could be relied upon to provide much coveted fresh venison and buffalo humps and tongues to the crews and passengers of the steamers. To escape detec-tion of the marauding Sioux, Dauphin's technique to deliver meat was to seclude himself in the brush, emerging from cov-er as a steamer approached. In 1863, Captain LaBarge piloted the heavily laden steamer *Robert Campbell,* destined for Fort Benton. Dauphin intercepted LaBarge a few miles before an impending Sioux ambush, sounding a warning. Perhaps be-cause of Dauphin's hunting skills or his knowledge of the tribes, his name was given to the worst barrier to navigating the Upper Missouri. An honor of sorts!

The volume of water determined the difficulty of passing the rapids. High water required the anchoring of dead men. Low water exposed snags and rocks. At times the scenes at the foot of the rapids appeared as semi- organized chaos: lines of boats and piles of freight, pilots haggling with wood hawks, wagons loaded with freight moving overland to the head of the rapids, disgruntled passengers milling about on shore.

The approach to Dauphin Rapids was guarded by shoals at Grand and Cow islands. These shoals were a warm-up call for the difficulties anticipated upriver. It was frequently required to off load all or a portion of a steamboat's freight to facilitate passage over the shoals, and then struggle up river to the foot of Dauphin, where additional freight was unloaded. Light-

Collapsing river banks were another ever-changing hazard on the Upper Missouri. A deep channel next to a high bank one day could be filled in by a dirt slide the next day as the powerful, abrasive river slashed at the bank. Here the steamboat Josephine *and the smaller steamboat* Little Jo *work to clear a dirt slide from the channel just below the "Cracon du Nez" (Bridge on the Nose) Rapids, about nine miles below Fort Benton.* OVERHOLSER HISTORICAL RESEARCH CENTER, FORT BENTON.

ened, the steamer would return to the shoals and retrieve the stored cargo. Finally reloaded, the steamer would attack Dauphin Rapids.

When water levels were extraordinary low and the rapids impassable even for an empty steamer, the stacked freight would be hauled overland by freight wagons to the head of the rapids, and after negotiating a contract, the freight would be repacked onboard steamers moored there. These steamers would take the freight and passengers to Fort Benton. Some vessels worked the circuit between the head of Dauphin and Fort Benton exclusively.

The difficulties faced by steamboats at Dauphin Rapids is best described by a personal observation from the wheelhouse of the 100-foot-long *Bertha*, traveling from Sioux City, Iowa, to Fort Benton. She made four trips to Fort Benton from 1868 and 1870. An unnamed passenger recorded one trip: "Friday, July 31, 1868 Twenty-four days out. Departed at peep of day. Ran up to Bird's Rapids (river mile 115), struck rapids, finally got over. Next bluff is a huge rock above the coolie that usually makes a break. Now it is four or five feet out of water. We do not run any distance without striking rocks. Weather cool. River stationary. Have had no mosquitoes for several nights. Got on a rock at the foot of Bear's Rapids. Captain went contrary to advice of engineer and laid line to right shore, after sparing over some huge rocks she started for the right shore and brought up on some large rocks, got off and sounded. Came over, rubbed and bumped around terribly, got over at dinner time. We strike rocks nearly every boat's length we go. Arrived at Dauphin's 6 p.m., sounded and put out warp, found thirty inches, went into it, but she did not get to the shoal water. In sparing her around a rock came through, water was over her timbers two or three times.

"Saturday, August 1, 1868 About 2 a.m. we got into the left shore and began putting out freight. About 6 a.m. the *Leoni Leoti* came down, put out a line and dropped through. She says *Success* was at Drowned Man's rapids thirty-four (actually 18 miles above) at dark last night, and the *Leoni Leoti* reports only twenty-two inches here at Dauphin's. Her pilot, Mr. Jacobs, says the *Success* found thirty inches, same as we did. We put out nearly all of our freight (three or four yawl loads) an left shore and cordelled it up to left point above the rapids. We succeeded in getting her a little further up than she was last night, but rubbed very hard on the rocks, broke our wheel badly, dead man pulled up or broke in two and we were compelled to drop into shore. Sounded left chute, two feet, laid up.

"Sunday, August 2, 1868 Weather beautiful. River fell one inch last night. We are still at the bank. Cleaned our boilers last night. *Andrew Ackley* came down about 9:30 a.m. and landed on left shore above rapids. Her passengers walked down to the *Leoni Leoti*, she left as soon as all were on board. We made arrangements with the *Ackley* to take our freight to Fort Benton for 1 ¼ cents per pound. She came down over the rapids about 10:30 a.m., got the freight on board, also the passengers, and started up about 6 p.m., went up without a line, struck some rocks. Atkins and Sims went up to the freight pile above the rapids. We bade all our friends adieu and returned to our boat after dark. *Ackley* leaves at daylight for Benton and we for Sioux City. God speed to both." (*Montana's Wild and Scenic Upper Missouri*)

Steamboats were temperamental vessels, subject to sudden violence. Fate could intervene with deadly consequences. The steamboat *Big Hatchie's* boiler blew up near Herman, Missouri, in 1845, killing 35 people. The pilot and clerk aboard the *Timour* were blown to pieces by an exploding boiler while taking on wood near Jefferson City. Passengers viewing the river from a bluff above the steamer escaped injuries when the boat's safe catapulted into their midst.

The disaster that occurred at a spit of land above Lexington, Missouri, in 1852 went down as the worst in the history of steam travel on the "Big Muddy." On Wednesday, April 7, Captain Francis T. Belt prepared to pilot the steamer *Saluda* through a channel of ominous, muddy water, littered with miniature icebergs. The steamer's twin engines and double boilers failed to breach the current after repeated attempts. The laboring engines and crashing chunks of ice forced Belt to pause, anchor off Lexington, and ascertain the situation.

The *Saluda's* lower deck housed a number of Mormon immigrants bound for Salt Lake Valley. They were becoming belligerent about the delay and the cold conditions. The next morning Belt again tried the current, but again he was forced to retreat to Lexington. Rankled by the discontented bellyaching of the passengers and that his reputation as an elite riverboat captain was coming under scrutiny from a crowd gathering on shore, he decided to force the issue.

In the early morning of April 9, Belt ordered his engineer to lock down the safety valve and reportedly said, "Fill her fire boxes. I want more steam. I'm going to round that point or blow her to hell trying." The *Saluda* had moved but a few yards from her moorings, gathering momentum, when the boilers exploded. The bow of the boat disintegrated into a cloud of splinters, some as small as match sticks, some the size of tree trunks. Human corpses and body parts mixed with the wreckage of the boiler, the hurricane decks, and the wheelhouse. The twin iron smoke stacks shot skyward like launched rockets. People left alive on the remaining part of the hull were scalded with boiling steam, their screams heard by spectators on shore. Captain Belt's macerated, dead body flew through the air like a rag doll shot from a cannon, landing on a bluff above the river. The steamer's 600-pound iron safe and the body of clerk Jonathan Blackburn arched through the sky, coming to earth 200 yards from the river. Two apprentice pilots in the wheelhouse were impaled with splinters and catapulted into the river, their bodies never recovered. Casualties on shore include one person cut in half by a flying boiler plate, and a brick house, struck by a cannon ball-like piece of boiler, collapsed.

Onlookers rushed to the scene, finding devastation resembling a battlefield. Limbs, torsos, and unidentifiable body parts were scattered about. Bloodied, dazed, and incoherent survivors screamed in agony, some calling for relatives. More than 100 bodies—more or less— were recovered. An unknown number of bodies were swept downstream, hidden beneath muddy currents and interred in the silty bottom. The remaining pieces of the hull sank just off shore. Fifty persons survived what was the worst disaster in the history of steamboat travel on the Missouri.

Father Pierre-Jean De Smet, a Jesuit priest who traveled to the Upper Missouri to minister to the Indians, had crossed the Atlantic Ocean four times. He observed that he feared the sea, but he said all the storms and unpleasant things he had experienced on the ocean crossings did not inspire him with as much terror as did his steamboat travel on the somber, treacherous, muddy Missouri.

CHAPTER 16

Steamer Bertrand: Time Capsule

OVER DECADES, NUMEROUS STEAMERS were lost plying the waters of the Missouri from its juncture with the Mississippi to Fort Benton: boiler explosions, fires, disembowelment by rocks and snags, crushed by ice, or collisions with sturdy railroad bridges—even torn apart by tornadoes. In less than 30 years, 400 steamboats were claimed by the unforgiving Missouri. In most instances, large percentages of the cargos were removed from the wrecked boat at the time; in others, cargos were salvaged years later; and in others, cargos remain imprisoned in layers of silt and mud.

On April Fool's Day, 1865, the Missouri claimed another victim, and its remains were preserved by a number of unique natural phenomena, like the fossilized skeleton of a dinosaur. While en route to Fort Benton, the 161-foot *Bertrand*, carrying 251 tons of freight, plowed into a minefield of snags 25 miles above Omaha, Nebraska. At an acute bend in the river, she was speared by an unforeseen log oscillating a few inches below the opaque surface. In minutes, the steamer sank in a few feet of water. All passengers were ferried to shore, but a treasure trove of 19th-century artifacts sank into the ooze with the hull.

Built in 1864 by businessmen living in Wheeling, Virginia, the *Bertrand*, known as a "packet" steamer, carried both passengers and freight. The boat, light for her class and able to navigate in 18 inches of water when empty, was not ostentatious. Although built primarily to carry big tonnages of freight, the vessel's design provided reasonable accommodations for passengers, crew, and officers. The captain, clerk, and two engineers would have been quartered in facilities apart from the other crew members. Vessels similar to the *Bertrand* would also have crewed a chambermaid and cook, who were housed in upscale cabins if the boat lacked a full complement of passengers. Toilet facilities were open holes passing down through the deck, opening over the paddlewheel. The "convenience holes" also served as depositories for dirty laundry water. It has been estimated there were about 20 first-class passengers on board at the time of her sinking. It must be noted that the physical evidence of the *Bertrand*'s cargo is well documented, but reports and records of the *Bertrand*'s physical appearance and crew remain open to educated guesses. There is little doubt she was designed for use in shallow water, perhaps for use on the Ohio River during times of low water. There is no conclusive evidence she was intended solely for the rugged conditions experienced by mountain boats on the Upper Missouri.

Over the years the *Bertrand*'s hull became buried in silt, and the river channel meandered away, concealing the exact location of the vessel's grave. For decades, stories persisted about a fabulous treasure of gold, 5,000 gallons of whiskey, and 35,000 pounds of mercury (used to extract gold from ore) that lay buried in the hull. The engines, boilers, and machinery had been salvaged shortly after the sinking, leaving behind clothing, food and containers, farming and mining equipment, and thousands of personal items.

For more than a century, periodic searches had failed to locate the wreck. In 1968, treasure hunters sunk a 6-inch drill 28 feet through layers of silt and clay. The drill retrieved wood, the physical evidence that appeared to be boat planking. A huge pit was dug, promptly filling with groundwater. Then an elaborate system of piping and pumps cleared the excavation, revealing the outline of a vessel's hull. From the boat's storage compartments a crate was found bearing the label "Bertrand." Confirmation was affirmed when a chalkboard was found with the name "Fannie" carved on its frame. Fannie Campbell was a child known to have been a passenger on the ill-fated steamer.

Fate entombed the *Bertrand's* contents in a hard, blue clay, sealing the hull and protecting an unusually large tonnage of freight from the corrosive effects of weather and atmosphere. The essentially anaerobic environment preserved in pristine condition the articles stored in the hull and the personal belongings of the crew and passengers. The more than 200,000 artifacts salvaged from the *Bertrand* give us a picture of what miners and settlers considered necessities in 1865.

The vessel's manifest included many familiar items used today, some perfectly preserved as if bottled or packaged yesterday: barrels of flour and nuts, jars of honey, catsup, mustard, cans of pineapple, and powdered lemonade. Bottles of medicinal alcohol and medicines have legible paper labels. Three-thousand pairs of shoes and boots, shirts and coats, ivory, brass, tin, lead, and bolts of silk were unearthed in near mint condition. Because the steamer sank so quickly, many personal items were abandoned: clocks, combs, lamps, mirrors, candy dishes, waffle irons, gloves, jewelry, and shawls. Crates of hammers, axes, doorknobs, washboards, plows, and sleigh bells were found. Pick axes and blasting powder destined for the goldfields were recovered.

Speculation indicates the main deck may have been occupied by other freight such as cattle or horses that could not be carried in the hold. Horses and cattle were in demand in Montana at the time, commanding good prices.

To date the unearthing of the *Bertrand* is the single known example of the near intact remains of a Missouri steamer, its cargo, and personal possessions of the passengers and crew, to be professionally examined, cataloged, and displayed. Today visitors can see hundreds of the articles salvaged from the *Bertrand* at the DeSoto National Wildlife Refuge in Missouri Valley, Iowa.

Author's note: I have personally visited the displayed artifacts recovered from the Bertrand and highly recommend visiting the expansive exhibits.

CHAPTER 17

Steamboat Captains: Daring and Determined

CAPTAINS (ALSO KNOWN AS "PILOTS") were at the top of a steamboat's pecking order. They were highly regarded professionals, commanding high salaries and prestige. They were men of strong character, who exercised complete authority over crews and passengers, yet were charming and socially accomplished. With astute business savvy, captains who owned their own steamers could manipulate shippers, merchants, and wood hawks, gaining economic advantage.

Navigation demanded constant vigilance. Without beacons, buoys, or reliable maps, learning to "read" the river channel became an essential skill, requiring intense focus for prolonged periods of time. Instantaneous decisions with minimal margins of error had to be made: avoiding rocks, charting rapids and sandbars, identifying floating debris and snags, judging the direction and force of winds, and finding scarce fuels. Critical water levels could vary from day to day, necessitating frequent sounding under the bow and stern, and river channels and obstacles could change from one season to the next, requiring a risky relearning of the best routes. Some hazards were transitory, here today and gone tomorrow. The Missouri earned a reputation as one of the most difficult rivers in the world to travel safely.

Sandbars were particularly problematic. The depth of opaque water covering tongues of sand extending into the river could not be easily estimated, so captains had to make split-second decisions to power over them, or not. One passenger noted: "Navigating the Missouri is like putting a steamer on dry land and sending a boy ahead with a sprinkling pot." Night travel entailed significant risks, but some daring pilots ran the lower river at night, navigating by moonlight and by the echoes of their steam whistles.

In general, steamboat captains were noted as daring risk takers, but however bold, most captains, weighing profit potential against the vagarious nature of the river, chose not to overload their boats. Those who arrived at Fort Benton with cargo intact secured the best profits.

A riverboat captain had to multi-task in the extreme. They had to memorize hundreds of mid-river and on-shore landmarks so they could estimate distances and time traveled, thereby estimating arrival times at destinations. The captain dictated how cargo was to be packed in the hull. Transporting extra tonnage meant a more profitable trip, but extra weight required more water under the hull. Cargo also had to be arranged in sequential order according to the stops made at camps and settlements along the river. Along the way, pilots had to manage ticklish negotiations with Indians, unreliable machinery, and disgruntled passengers.

In addition to all the other challenges, the pilot had to rule with absolute authority a crew of rough-hewn, uneducated men, sometimes picked randomly from the docks or camps as the need arose. Men performing hard labor and suffering poor accommodations, low pay, and often inferior rations chaffed under the tough, aggressive management style of the pilots, but it was the only way to maintain order and keep the boat operating smoothly.

The advantages of steamboat travel were profound, but if a boat wrecked, the financial consequences were enormous, putting boat owners and freight companies in financial jeopardy, not to mention the emotional distress and inconvenience suffered by passengers.

The most accomplished, adaptable captains were in demand by merchants and boat builders, and they were handsomely rewarded for their services, some commanding salaries as high as $1500 a month, a princely sum for the time. The two most notable men to captain steamers on the Missouri were Joseph LaBarge and Grant Marsh. They possessed exemplary strength of character, earning reputations as men with exceptional talent and possessing acumen and cool heads in time of crisis. They had the faculty of quickly assessing situations without conscious reasoning.

Joseph Marie LaBarge

CAPTAIN JOSEPH MARIE LABARGE was a handsome, dynamic man of French-Canadian heritage. He was recognized by his peers as having no equal at working a steamer through unfamiliar channels with his intuitive, uncanny ability to feel with his feet and hear with his ears the mood of his vessel and the river's disposition. His competence and acceptance of challenge tempered with calculated risk made him in demand.

At 17, LaBarge traveled into the Rockies with Pierre Chouteau's American Fur Company. He became a fur trader and learned the stoic nature of the Indians, gaining confidence in dealing with the native's mercurial temperaments. In 1832, while still engaged in the fur trade, LaBarge began learning about steamboat travel while on a trip upriver aboard the

As a young man Joseph Marie LaBarge went west for the fur trade and saw a future in steamboats. He worked his way up to captain and bought his first steamboat when he was 31 years old. He became of the most celebrated pilots on the upper river, admired for his uncanny ability to navigate the river's treacherous channels.

American Fur Company's steamer *Yellowstone*. As the fur trade began to wane, LaBarge, seeing economic advantage in the infant steamboat business, abandoned the fur trade and became a steamboat clerk. He soon got noticed for his work ethic, honesty, and quick mind. Promoted to the wheelhouse as an apprentice steersman, he quickly advanced to pilot on the less challenging Lower Missouri. In 1846, at 31 years of age, he bought the steamer *General Brooks* for $12,000. Adept at making money, he built up a good sum by buying boats in need of repairs and then selling them at a profit.

LaBarge was known and trusted by many of the Indian chiefs along the river, and he understood the tribes better than the Army officers and agents who were responsible for dealing with them. This trait became increasingly important as the tribes of the Upper Missouri became increasingly dependent on government annuities (often called peace bribes): shipments of food, metal implements, and clothing. The Indians became sullen and disgruntled when annuities fell short of promises, with many annuities being stolen by unscrupulous Indian agents and traded to the highest bidder. LaBarge, with a stage presence, mediated many confrontations to the satisfaction of all parties.

However, in at least one instance LaBarge threatened violence to defuse a tense standoff. In 1847, while piloting the *Martha*, he docked at Crow Creek in the Dakota Territory. His mission included delivering annuities to the Sioux. Only part of the allotted sugar, coffee, tobacco, and clothing were unloaded, causing indignation among the natives, who fired a volley into the steamer, killing one crewman. The Sioux forced their way across the gangplank onto the steamer, crowding through the forward passageways, attempting to take over the boat. Unfamiliar with the layout of the vessel,

Captain Joseph LaBarge stands on the upper deck of the De-Smet *at the Fort Benton Levee circa 1873. LaBarge captained several Upper Missouri steamboats in his 50-year career. He was the subject of an important two-volume book entitled* History of Early Steamboat Navigation on the Missouri River – The Life and Adventures of Joseph LaBarge *by Hiram Chittenden, published in 1903.* OVERHOLSER HISTORICAL RESEARCH CENTER, FORT BENTON.

the invaders hesitated, prompting the quick-thinking LaBarge into action. Knowing the Indians great fear of the grape-shot-spewing brass cannon, the captain maneuvered the *Martha's* deck gun into position, and by signs indicated he would blow the invaders to the "happy hunting ground" if they didn't immediately abandon the boat. Mortified, pushing past one another in their haste, the Indians vacated the boat.

Despite his admirable traits, LaBarge ignored the federal

ban on selling whiskey to the tribes and developed crafty strategies to cash in on the lucrative trade. He was adept at outfoxing federal inspectors, unloading barrels of whiskey, mixed and hidden with other cargo, only to be returned on board after the inspector had certified the boat clean, or pushing stocks of whiskey ahead of inspectors crawling around the confining recesses of a dark hold.

One problem that steamer captains had little control over, and did not understand, was infectious, frequently fatal, communicable diseases, especially cholera and smallpox. Inherently, the fetid environment of a vessel crowded with people from all corners of the East was an incubator for disease. With no escape options, frightened passengers and crew had to remain onboard, hoping for the best. In 1851, LaBarge, while piloting the *St. Ange*, had his ship swept by a cholera epidemic that infected more than 100 passengers and crew, killing 11.

As the fur trade gave way to the gold trade, LaBarge's quick mind moved from profits in the uncertain and illegal whiskey trade to the astronomical legal remunerations to be made by supplying the tens of thousands of gold miners and immigrants rushing west. Markups of 100 or 200 percent on delivered merchandise were common.

In 1864, LaBarge, by virtue of his honesty and reputation for decency, gathered enough cash to purchase the controlling interest in the steamer *Effie Deans*. Destined for Fort Benton, he piloted a varied cargo of goods up river, including whiskey (for saloon use), mining tools, food, clothing, and tobacco. Low water stopped him short of Fort Benton, but he managed to gather teams of oxen, freight wagons, and drivers to take his cargo to Fort Benton in time for the summer and fall mining seasons. After making arrangements for the return of the *Effie Deans* to St. Louis, LaBarge sold some goods in Fort

The steamer Josephine *is moored below LaBarge Rock on the Upper Missouri. The striking landmark in the White Cliffs section of the Wild and Scenic Upper Missouri River was named after Captain Joseph LaBarge.* Murphy Library Special Collections, University of Wisconsin-La Crosse.

Benton and then transported the remainder to Virginia City, Montana. Citizens, merchants, and miners eagerly bought his wares at the usual inflated prices, rewarding LaBarge with $100,000 in gold dust. He evaded a series of mishaps with road agents and Indians, returning to St. Louis via Salt Lake City and the Platte River. A year later, the *Effie Deans*, while tied to the dock at St. Louis, was consumed by fire, ending LaBarge's career as a steamer captain. He remained an influential sage on steamboat travel on the Missouri well into his 70s. He was a man to be emulated, and he died a person of renown in 1899 at the age of 84.

Grant Marsh

In June 1866, 31 steamers were laboring upstream to Fort Benton, all competing to be the first to unload tons of food stuffs and mining equipment of every description. One of those steamers, the *Luella*, was piloted by a new captain, Grant Marsh. The 34-year-old had never been on the Upper Missouri, but on June 17 Marsh landed the *Luella* at Fort Benton's half-mile-long levee. It was a remarkable accomplishment, but Marsh had more daring plans.

In the late spring and early summer it was common practice for captains to hurry downriver after unloading cargo at Fort Benton to avoid becoming marooned by falling river levels. Reasoning that many miners would quit the diggings in the fall and be anxious to return downriver to hearth and home in the East, Marsh made a dangerous decision to stay. He worked the Upper Missouri well into August, ferrying passengers and freight that had grounded on shoals and sandbars downriver from Fort Benton. He would pilot the empty *Luella* downriver, stopping above an impassable rapid. Cargo unloaded from a steamer stranded below the rapid would be freighted by ox-drawn wagons to the *Luella*, reloaded, and transported to Fort Benton.

By early September, the *Luella* was the only vessel tied to the Fort Benton levee, and miners were gathering in some numbers. They paid for the downstream voyage in gold dust and nuggets. Secured in leather pouches or in money belts buckled around waists was $1,250,000 of the precious metal, the most lucrative single shipment ever to travel down the Missouri. By innate, intuitive abilities and secure in personal confidence, Marsh successfully navigated low-water shoals

Historians have often referred to Grant Marsh as the best steam-boat captain on the Upper Missouri and Yellowstone rivers. He started his steamboat career in 1856 as a cabin boy and eventually become a pilot, captain, and owner. Over his 20-year career on the two rivers, his skill and daring became legendary.

and sandbars deemed impossible by lesser pilots. Not only did he earn a profit of $24,000, but he gained a seldom accorded degree of admiration from his peers.

Marsh had crewed on the steamer *John J. Roe* when it supported General Grant's forces at the Battle of Shiloh in 1862, and he foresaw the profits to be made filling government contracts to deliver annuities to the Indians and delivering supplies to the isolated military posts along the Upper Missouri. Later, recognized by the government as a competent, reliable steamer captain, he successfully piloted the steamers *Luella* and *Ida Stockdale* through riverbank ambushes by the Sioux while meeting military commitments.

Marsh enhanced his reputation with the military when the government, anxious to appease Red Cloud, the combative chief of the Oglala Sioux, asked Marsh to deliver the annually pledged payments of food and supplies. The request was unprecedented, because the annuities, in order to maintain peace, had to be delivered to the mouth of the Grand River in Dakota Territory by the end of October. Not only would Marsh and his crew have to pilot the steamer *Nile* through extremely low water but also risk the real possibility of becoming trapped and crushed in ice. No doubt, Marsh's ego, a desire to demonstrate his skills as a steamer pilot, and the lure of lucrative military contracts in the future enticed Marsh to accept the challenge.

Low water forced Marsh to abandon his cargo on an island short of Grand River and beat a hasty retreat down river. The *Nile* made less than 100 miles before sharp chunks of ice scraped and battered her hull, risking a punctured hull. Forced to moor the vessel in a protected backwater, the vessel and crew were the first to survive ice-bound in the Missouri until spring breakup. The Army was duly impressed by Marsh's effort.

1881.   OLD RELIABLE   1881.

COULSON LINE

(Our Refference—THE GREAT WEST.)

S. B. COULSON,   **J. C. McVAY,**
Gen. Manager.   Gen. Frt. and Ticket Agt.

OPERATING AND CONTROLLING

The Largest, Finest and Best Equipped Steamers on
the Western Waters; built expressly for the

Missouri and Yellowstone Rivers,

Will operate during the season of 1881 between Bismarck and Fort Benton and Bismarck and all
points on the Yellowstone.

Steamers will Positively Leave as Advertised.

In addition to his navigation skills, Captain Marsh was a keen businessman. He bought and sold steamboats, and he became a partner in the Coulson Line which operated several steamboats on the Yellowstone and Missouri rivers. This advertisement for the Coulson Line in 1881 boasts "the largest, finest, and best-equipped steamers on the western waters."

Over the years Marsh delivered cargo, mail, and fresh foods to isolated military posts, accepting navigational challenges deemed foolhardy by other steamer captains. For his services, the government paid Marsh the unheard-of sum of $1,200 per month. (During the 1860s, at the height of the steamer era, pilot/captains were earning salaries on average of $725 a month.) Through frugality and shrewd investments, Marsh became a partner in a steamboat enterprise known as the Coulson Packet Line, which greatly enhanced his earning potential and reputation. His contacts with the Army resulted in lucrative charters for Coulson Packet Line vessels, becoming the Army's "go-to company." Transporting troops and supplies for the Army, as well as fulfilling private contracts between St. Louis and Fort Benton, provided Marsh a comfortable life.

By the mid-1870s, the discovery of gold in the Black Hills of South Dakota increased the influx of whites into Indian territories, exacerbating the destruction of native cultures. The remaining free-roaming tribes were squeezed into the rich hunting grounds in and around the Yellowstone River. The threat of tribal territorial clashes was understood by Lieutenant General Phillip Sheridan of Civil War fame, who commanded forts on the frontier. He therefore deemed it prudent to explore the nature of the unknown country up the Yellowstone in anticipation of armed conflict with the belligerent, hard-pressed Sioux.

The military often requested that Captain Marsh personally undertake the most perilous projects. In 1873, Sheridan tapped Marsh to navigate the here-to-for unchartered Yellowstone River. His orders to chart the Yellowstone to the mouth of the Powder River, a distance of 400 miles, was an assignment uncertain of success. In any season the Yellowstone River carried a fraction of the water found in the Missouri, and by late May, spring runoff had already passed. Undaunted, Marsh nudged the bow of the *Key West* into the narrow channel of the Yellowstone at its juncture with the Missouri River near the Montana-North Dakota border.

One can only speculate the trepidation suffered by Marsh. He had assembled a hand-picked crew, but no one knew if the Yellowstone was navigable for more than a few miles above its confluence with the Missouri. Becoming stranded on a gravel bar would compromise Marsh's reputation, sacrifice the *Key West*, and endanger the crew.

After penetrating some distance upriver, it became difficult to gather cottonwood in sufficient quantity to feed the voracious boilers. The problem was solved by harvesting great piles of driftwood. After laboriously sparing and warping through innumerable interlocking mazes of shallows and rock reefs, and inching through narrow channels, the recalcitrant Yellowstone River submitted. With resolute fearlessness, Marsh piloted the *Key West* to the mouth of the Powder River and returned to the Missouri in just 9 days, without serious injury to crew or vessel. Marsh meticulously recorded landmarks and areas of the channel that required special diligence, providing valuable references for future navigation.

In the mid-1870s, U.S. Army Lieutenant Colonel George Custer and the troops under his command were ordered to guard a group of surveyors for the Northern Pacific Railroad who were plotting a rail line up the Yellowstone River valley. Marsh, the logical choice to provide supply support for the 7th Calvary, again nosed his vessel into the Yellowstone. The voyage, again successful, provided Marsh with yet more knowledge of the river.

General Sheridan, increasingly anxious about the tribes gathering in considerable numbers in the areas of the Tongue and Bighorn Rivers (tributaries of the Yellowstone), thought it judicious to consider establishing a permanent military presence in the area. Sending the steamer *Josephine* with 100 fully armed soldiers and a rapid-firing Gatling gun into the heart of the Indian stronghold would send a strong message, so Sheridan ordered Marsh to ascend the Yellowstone hundreds of miles farther upstream than he had gone.

To put a maximum amount of water under the keel, Marsh guided the *Josephine* into the Yellowstone during spring snowmelt. Filled bank to bank, the depth of the frothing,

Grant Marsh served aboard more than 20 vessels in his long career. Many of his trips were as captain of the Josephine, *shown here. In 1875, contracted by U.S. Army to see how far steamboats could travel up the Yellowstone River, Marsh navigated the* Josephine *to near present-day Livingston, Montana. No other steamboat ever went that far up the Yellowstone.* Montana Historical Society Research Center Photograph Archives, Helena, Montana.

wave-crested river sufficiently flooded the sand and gravel bars, enabling Marsh to pilot the *Josephine* to the mouth of the Power River without having to set her spars even once, avoiding delays. At Powder River, Marsh rested his crew and inspected his vessel in preparation to penetrate the unknown hazards of the Upper Yellowstone.

The landmarks— rocky channels, driftwood piles, midstream islands, acute river bends— between the Powder and Bighorn rivers were meticulously charted by Marsh. Verdant, timbered islands and notable rock outcroppings were named in honor of military personnel or spouses or notable characters of the era. Steaming up the pulsating channel, the men marveled at the massive herds of buffalo and elk grazing in the river bottoms, and hunters kept the crew supplied with buffalo tongues and hump meat. The long summer days continued sunny and mild. For exercise, some men explored on foot, harvesting wild plums, cherries, and currents. Occasionally, deserted Indian encampments were found, some with cooking fires still smoldering. Pushing his luck upon reaching the mouth of the Bighorn River, Marsh dared to nose the *Josephine* into the smaller river, exploring a few miles upriver, logging more valuable information, before returning to the Yellowstone.

Two days travel above the confluence of the Bighorn, the Yellowstone River compressed into a tight channel between high, vertical cliffs. Once committed to the channel, there was no escape. Marsh, demonstrating his brash, confident character, plunged his crew and vessel into the millrace, putting the expedition at great risk. While deck hands toiled mightily with spars and capstans, the steamer, nearly bursting its boilers, inched forward, gradually overcoming the torrent. Reaching calmer water, the *Josephine* came abreast of Pompey's Pillar (50 miles east of present-day Billings, Montana). The sandstone butte was named in honor of Pompey, the child of the Lewis and Clark Expedition's Shoshone guide, Sacagawea. Clark carved his name in the sandstone on his return to the United States via the Yellowstone River on July, 25, 1806. It is the only known physical evidence that remains from the famous journey. The historic landmark was thought unreachable by steamer.

Continuing upriver, the terrain, almost imperceptibly, gained elevation, rising toward the Continental Divide, causing the *Josephine*'s engines to labor near the breaking point against a quickening current. The vessel's tall stacks belched black smoke; the paddlewheel churned a frothy wake; the hull creaked and twisted; but no amount of warping, sparing, and a frenzied crew could gain more than 53 miles. On June 7, 1875, Marsh was stopped by a rapids generating 5-foot waves and sucking whirlpools near present-day Livingston, Montana, just 60 miles from the northern border of Yellowstone National Park—a 483-mile voyage never to be repeated by a steamer.

In early June the Yellowstone River was still in full spring runoff, and in many ways the return voyage created an entirely different set of navigational problems for Marsh, requiring near magical skills. Controlling the momentum of a vessel propelled by a swift current requires diligence more precise than a slow, calculated advance against the current. One stratagem Marsh used was to reverse the paddlewheel, slowing the vessel as it entered a stretch of bad water. This gave Marsh more control and let him more accurately choose the least hazardous course. Despite the difficulties, high water sufficiently shielded the vessel's hull from submerged rocks and the *Josephine* covered 100 miles or more daily, reaching the Missouri in four days.

Grant Marsh had accomplished the seemingly impossible. He was the only steamboat captain with an intimate knowledge of the Yellowstone River. No one knew the 1875 journey was a dress rehearsal for a feat that would propel the stalwart captain to national prominence.

The next year General Phil Sheridan asked Marsh to undertake a special duty, to which Marsh readily agreed. Marsh arrived at Fort Abraham Lincoln across the river from Bismarck, North Dakota, on May 27, 1876, ten days after the departure of the 7th Calvary. His mission was to load sup-

Grant Marsh piloted the steamer Far West, *shown here, during the Indian Wars of the 1870s, and both the captain and the boat made history. The* Far West *was built for the Coulson Line in 1870 in Pittsburgh, Pennsylvania. It was 189 feet long and 33.5 feet wide. Its single stern paddlewheel measured 19 feet in diameter and 23.5 feet in width. The boat cost $24,000, about $400,000 in value today.* MURPHY LIBRARY SPECIAL COLLECTIONS, UNIVERSITY OF WISCONSIN-LA CROSSE.

Set for dinner, the dining room of the Far West *was impressive with comfortable chairs, tablecloths, fine place settings, and kerosene-lamp chandeliers. The long room could be divided into separate dining areas by a curtain.* OVERHOLSER HISTORICAL RESEARCH CENTER, FORT BENTON.

plies—grain for the horses, hard tack and dried meat for the men, extra tents, spare rifle parts, medical supplies, and thousands of rounds of small arms ammunition—sufficient to support the troops as he paralleled their movements as closely as possible via the Yellowstone River. In the event of deadly action, Marsh would be expected to provide logistical support, like a floating, mobile supply depot and hospital ship.

General Alfred Terry commanded the U.S. Army column during the Indian Wars of 1876 and 1877. He often contracted steamboats to transport soldiers and supplies on the Yellowstone and Missouri rivers. Grant Marsh was the Army's preferred steamboat captain.

Staying close to the action would be problematic, as coordinating the whereabouts of the troops and the steamer would be tenuous at best.

Marsh considered the 190-foot stern wheeler *Far West*, chartered by the Army for $360 a day from the Coulson's Packet Companies fleet of steamers, the most suitable for the whims of the Yellowstone. Loaded with cargo, she needed a scant 30 inches of water under her hull to glide over shoals and sandbars. His handpicked crew consisted of 30 experienced deck hands and two trusted engineers to oversee the *Far West's* boilers and powerful engines. Sixty soldiers, providing security, were taken on board during a layover at Fort Buford.

On June 7th, 1876, Custer and his column rendezvoused with Marsh at the mouth of the Powder River. On June 21, General Terry held a council of war aboard the *Far West*. A grand plan to trap the encamped Indians in a pincer movement was decided. The next day, Custer, true to his impetuous, ambitious personality, hastily prepared sufficient horses, pack mules, supplies, and troops. Wanting to make speed by eliminating any encumbrances, Custer left behind on the *Far West* the three Gatling guns and extra soldiers. He only allowed his men a scant 15 days of rations and a paucity of 50 extra rounds of ammunition. He led the troops at a hurried pace up the drainage of Rosebud Creek toward destiny.

Two days after Custer's departure, Marsh's crew ferried Colonel Gibbon and his cavalry troop across the Yellowstone. They rode south to coordinate the attack on Crazy Horse and the Indian camp. A day later, a messenger whipping a lathered horse delivered orders from Gibbon. With all haste, Marsh was to immediately ascend the Yellowstone and pilot the *Far West* up the Bighorn River. The purpose was to maintain reasonably close contact with the advancing troops.

On June 21, 1876, General Terry held a council of war aboard the Far West, *moored on the Yellowstone River. The next day, Lt. Colonel George Armstrong Custer, shown here, and his troops left the* Far West *and rode to their destiny on the Little Bighorn River. Because of his haste to travel light and fast, Custer left three rapid-fire Gatling guns and extra ammunition aboard the* Far West. LIBRARY OF CONGRESS.

The Bighorn, even though swollen with spring runoff, would be a daunting challenge: a ribbon of water more shallow, sinuous, and narrow than the Yellowstone. Nosing the steamer into the mouth of the Bighorn, Marsh, to his dismay, soon met foaming rapids sweeping around numerous midstream islands, requiring the captain and his crew to squeeze the steamer between rocky shores and islands stacked with log jams piled like jack-straws.

Marsh devised an untried technique. Using the narrowness of the river channel to advantage, he crept the steamer upstream. Deck hands, guarded by armed infantry, were put ashore, fastening heavy ropes to cottonwood trees or boulders on both banks. The ropes were wrapped around paired, bow-mounted, steam-powered capstans, rotated by the *Far West*'s powerful engines. The mechanical advantage of winching, coordinated with incessant sparing, slowly lifted the steamer over innumerable rock gardens and sandbars. Infrequent stretches of open water demanded the process be repeated every few hundred yards.

The brute physical labor and the June heat pushed the crew's endurance to the limit, but curtains of smoke from hundreds of Indian fires drifting across the distant horizon encouraged the men to superhuman efforts. One can only imagine the metallic clanking and banging of the vessel's engines under full power; the thrashing paddlewheel; the hissing steam; black smoke belching from paired stacks; and the grunting, sweating, swearing men on shore repeatedly re-anchoring heavy ropes. The noise and choreographed confusion of muscling the cumbersome vessel against the current would have been a noteworthy sight.

Despite the difficulties, Marsh progressed up the Bighorn 50 miles in 36 hours to a point within 11 miles of the Indian's camp on the Little Bighorn River, a smaller tributary. The depth of the main river had dropped to less than three feet, so Marsh and his crew settled in to await developments. Soldiers were positioned to guard the steamer. Granted the opportunity to finally relax, a few well-armed crew members left the boat to fish or explore the island to which the *Far West* was anchored.

Suddenly, like a bad omen, an Indian riding hard on a lathered horse burst from the brush. Recognized as Curley, a Crow scout for Custer, he was brought on board. His startling appearance and demeanor sent a ripple of anxious murmurs through the gathering crew. Curley, using pencil and paper, sign language, and body and facial expressions, made his shocking news understood: Custer and the 7th Calvary had been exterminated to the last man. (Later it was learned the Curley, awed by the overwhelming number of armed Sioux, had fled at the onset of the battle).

At dawn the next morning, a soldier from Gibbon's troop, who had ridden all night searching for the *Far West*, reached the boat. He had first-hand knowledge about the catastrophic fate of Custer and the 7th Calvary. Dividing his force into three units, Custer attacked the Indians camp prematurely. Surrounded and vastly outnumbered, he made a stand and died in a hail of bullets and arrows along with the five companies under his command. The men from the other seven companies led by Major Reno and Captain Benteen had been pinned down on a barren, rocky hilltop for 36 hours before the Indians decamped and fled into the Bighorn Mountains. Nearly five dozen troopers were wounded. These survivors, many with life-threatening wounds, were being transported on stretchers to the *Far West*. They arrived three days after the battle.

A column of troops under the command of Colonel John Gibbon, shown here, discovered the bodies of "Custer's Last Stand" on June 26 and probably saved the lives of hundreds of troopers under the command of Major Marcus Reno, who were still under siege. Gibbon himself arrived the next day and helped evacuate the wounded to the steamboat Far West, *which Grant Marsh had managed to navigate a considerable distance up the Bighorn River, a shallow tributary of the Yellowstone, to provide closer support for the troops.*

On board the *Far West*, the wounded were placed on make-shift mattresses of freshly cut grass covered with blankets, converting the deck of the *Far West* into an improvised emergency room. Included among the retreating troops was Henry Porter, the sole survivor of three regimental doctors. Without Dr. Porter ministering to the wounded on the retreat and on the trip down the Yellowstone, many would not have survived.

The sights and groans of the troopers on his deck invoked a sense of urgency fully understood by Marsh. He ordered the *Far West* released from its mooring and called for power from the paired engines. The *Far West* turned into the current. The intrinsic difficulties of powering a 190-foot-long, three-story, apartment-building-sized steamer downstream in a swift current, maneuvering over rocks, rapids, and islands, were compounded by the narrowness of the Bighorn. To maintain reasonable rudder control over the direction of the boat, its speed had to be greater than the strength of the current, requiring split-second decisions to avoid smashing the steamer into rocks. Reversing the paddlewheels to slow the vessel proved impossible because of the sudden appearance of menacing underwater threats and the narrow channel's restrictions. The trek required constant vigilance and an uncanny ability to read the river, a river that no man had piloted downstream.

Marsh, his engineers, and firemen dashed the steamer an incredible 53 miles the first day, entering the Yellowstone River. Only one of the wounded troopers had expired. Because the balance of the wounded soldiers had somewhat stabilized, the steamer laid at anchor for two days, waiting to ferry the remainder of Gibbon's force, presently marching from the site of the battle, to safety on the north side of the Yellowstone River.

With the steamer the Far West, *shown here, Captain Grant Marsh made steamboat history—and secured his reputation as a peerless steamboat captain—when he transported wounded soldiers from the Battle of the Little Bighorn down the Yellowstone and Missouri rivers to Fort Abraham Lincoln at Bismarck, North Dakota, a distance of 710 river miles, in only 54 hours, a downstream speed record on the Missouri. In doing so, Marsh and the* Far West *brought the first news of "Custer's Massacre" to the nation.* MONTANA HISTORICAL SOCIETY RESEARCH CENTER PHOTOGRAPH ARCHIVES, HELENA, MONTANA.

Emboldened by his success at navigating the Bighorn and vivified by the role in which fate had cast him, Marsh and his crew seemingly flew the steamer down the wider but still treacherous Yellowstone. To run the river at night tempted fate, but Marsh, alternating four-hour shifts with second mate Dave Campbell, kept the *Far West* headed down current on the evening of June 30. Marsh had calculated the gamble, knowing that darkness did not envelope the northern plains until after 10 p.m. and the first streaks of pale light would tickle the horizon by 5:15 a.m., minimizing the hours exposed to unseen hazards.

Running maximum boiler pressure, Marsh pushed the steamer and its crew to the limit. The *Far West* glanced off islands and midstream rocks, jolting patients and crew and twisting the steamer's frame. The hull held together. Near midnight on July 5, 1876, Marsh reached Bismarck, Dakota Territory, across the Missouri from Fort Abraham Lincoln. Soon the news of "Custer's last stand" was telegraphed to the world.

Marsh had piloted the *Far West* 700 miles from the mouth of the Bighorn River to Bismarck in 54 hours, averaging a staggering 13 miles per hour, including stops for wood and the delay at Powder River. It was a record never beaten.

Guided by a belief in the power of daring and resolve, Captain Marsh piloted on western rivers for 22 years. He had the mental toughness to attempt difficult projects, and he thrived on risky drama. More than once he piloted uncertain channels to evade Indian ambushes. Nevertheless, it was the rescue of soldiers from the Battle of the Little Bighorn that secured Marsh's legend and his place in history.

CHAPTER 18

Crews: Rivermen and Roustabouts

STEAMER CREWS, INCLUDING ENGINEERS, roustabouts, mates, captains, clerks, and tradesmen, were an eclectic collection of American society, representing all socioeconomic strata. In all probability, men from the lower socio-economic class made steamboat travel on the Missouri possible because the physically demanding work was dangerous and not well paid. The exception to haphazard hiring practices was the engineer, whose responsibility revolved around monitoring boiler pressure and maintaining the paired piston engines. Other skilled positions include a blacksmith (a mechanical breakdown needed the attention a man with metallurgy experience), a carpenter (to repair warped decking and damaged hulls), a cook (it took considerable culinary skill to prepare palatable food before the advent of refrigeration), and a clerk.

The clerk possessed skills invaluable to the operation of a steamer. He was the official responsible for correspondence, records, and accounts. Freight manifests and values and documentation of wood purchases were meticulously recorded.

The lowliest of the laboring crew earned the ignominious title of roustabout (until the end of the Civil War, slaves were used as roustabouts, with their owners charging wages for their labor). After a 24-hour work day hauling bales, boxes, and mining equipment, they might catch a few hours' sleep while the steamer worked through a stretch of placid water. Their crude accommodations were the cargo room floor, sandwiched between barrels of flour or in hammocks strung from wooden beams. Ever on call for urgent duty, reasonable periods of restful sleep were never assured. The incessant clanging and banging of the engines and the vibrations and creaking of the wooden hull challenged sound sleep. The high-pressure engines exhausted steam with rhythmic blasts like the firing of cannons, another detriment to sleep. The artillery-like thunder could be heard for miles when the pilot called to the engineer through the "talking pipe" for more power.

Roustabouts were called to work at any hour. They were expected to carry cords of wood from shore to the vessel's deck over bouncing planks often slick with rain or ice. Roustabouts fell into social classes: Negro "roosters" accomplished the more onerous labor, German immigrants were trusted with more responsible duties, preteen and teenaged boys required a steady hand, and Irishmen were deemed unreliable, recalcitrant, and expendable. (In at least one instance, upon learning that a man had fallen overboard, the pilot was heard to say, "It's only an Irishman.")

The constant oversight of a crew could not be done by the engineer or captain. Their duties left little time to keep the crew on task. That task fell to the steamboat "mate," sort of a project manager. The vessel's mate, a large, deep-voiced imposing figure, drove a crew through intimidation and brute force, answering only to the captain. The more contemptuous controlled a crew with profanity, fists, and clubs. Some were even armed. Rumors circulated that a mutinous or trouble-making roustabout would be discretely dispatched, then conveniently committed to the muddy current.

The crew's food was wretched, often just leftovers from passenger fare piled into a common bowl. Rations of hard tack or salt pork were eaten on the run. Crew members occasionally went ashore to hunt the woodlots and coulees, harvesting buffalo or deer. Fresh meat, an uncommon treat, was usually divided among all aboard.

But a roustabout had some leverage. Demanding better conditions, crew members could desert a vessel on the eve of departure, or, simply wanting free passage to an upriver settlement, leave a boat short-handed. When a more lucrative employment presented itself, such as harvest work, a crew could refuse to take the steamer up river unless granted higher wages and improved food. Overall, a roustabout was an itinerant laborer. After receiving his pay in cash, a crew man might skip a trip or two up river, only to return after blowing his hard-earned money on the vices readily available in St. Louis.

If life on a steamer lacked refinement, it paid dividends in the daily viewing of world-class landscapes, endless buffalo herds, and enigmatic Indians. The sight of columns of black smoke belching from the twin stacks of a floating hotel with whistle blowing and engines cannonading must have thrilled the most callous mate. Pride and a sense of accomplishment must have been realized when a steamer, full of life-sustaining cargo, was hailed by cheering crowds at Fort Benton's levee. Surely, the most ignorant roustabout had some inkling that he was participating in an epic adventure.

One crew member had an uncommon, solitary duty. Individuals with hunting and shooting skills were hired by captains to provide fresh meat whenever the opportunity presented. Immense herds of buffalo were commonly seen grazing in close proximity to the river, as well as large numbers of deer and elk. The appearance of a group of buffalo caused a great commotion on board. Small boats filled with men eager for the chase, including the professional hunter, would be dispatched for the shore. Not all hunts ended happily. On one occasion the professional hunter, while alone, failed to return to the boat. A search by a group of well-armed men found his scalped and mutilated body full of arrows.

Experience, quick reflexes, and anticipation of risks saved men from falling overboard and drowning, or being cut in half by snapped cables or ropes, or being scalded by fractured steam pipes, or killed by boiler explosions and the resulting fires that could consume wooden structures in minutes. Notwithstanding the daily exposure to possible loss of life or limb, the demanding life of steamboat crews powering up the mighty Missouri was full of remarkable and exciting experiences.

CHAPTER 19

Passengers: Fortune-Seekers and Farmers

UNTIL THE CIVIL WAR, steamboats were cheaply constructed, imperfect vessels. Passenger space was limited and accommodations austere. Assaulted by incessant vibration and engine noise and the smell of smoke and engine oil, passengers slept on corn-husk mattresses on open decks, suffering the ravages of hordes of mosquitoes. Some passengers above deck shared small rooms. Some boats filled barrels with river water to satisfy thirsty or dirty passengers, while others simply fastened a bucket on a long rope. Exasperating, often long delays while repairing an engine or overcoming a stretch of submerged logs or sandbars were common and unforeseen.

Passengers to the Upper Missouri were an eclectic mix: the restless from low socio-economic populations, artists and scientists, European aristocrats, trappers and gold miners, and opportunistic entrepreneurs. Many kept journals or diaries. They were among the first to record the splendor of the river churned to froth by tens of thousands of migrating buffalo.

In 1866, John Napton staked a claim in Bear Gulch, Montana, and by September 1867 he had grubbed enough yellow metal to quit the country. At Fort Benton he joined a number of men who were anxious to return to the refinements of civilization. Three steamers waited at the levee, soliciting passen-

For steamboats on the Upper Missouri, it was usually more prof-itable to transport freight than to take passengers. But at times, passengers crowded the steamboats, especially miners heading to or from the gold strikes. Between 1877 and 1883, 17,000 pas-sengers were taken upriver and nearly 11,000 downriver. Here the Helena *poses with her passengers at Milk River Landing in 1880.* MONTANA HISTORICAL SOCIETY RESEARCH CENTER PHOTOGRAPH ARCHIVES, HELENA, MONTANA.

gers for St. Louis. Agents from the steamer *Imperial*, ground-ed by shallow water 100 miles downriver at Cow Island, were aggressively marketing cabin space. They convinced Napton that the *Imperial* offered sumptuous accommodations. Free transportation to Cow Island aboard mackinaws further en-ticed Napton to accept the solicitations. His impressions of the *Imperial* proved anything but luxurious. He described it as a "large stern-wheel boat but not very palatial in appear-ance." About 275 passengers had secured accommodations, paying an average of $130 in gold dust, but the decks of the *Imperial* only had space for half that number. "At night the whole cabin was filled with men rolled up in their blankets as thick as sardines in a box," Napton wrote. He gave further insight: "Although we made slow progress from the start, I never saw a happier, jollier crowd.... Here was truly a para-dise for game. Small herds of buffalo could be seen at a dis-tance on the prairies, and in the bottoms along the river. Elk and white-tailed deer were as thick as rabbits. Rocky Moun-tain sheep appeared constantly on the bluffs and along the riverbanks. The bears along here must have been as plentiful as in the time of Lewis and Clark. Everything gave promise of a prosperous and pleasant trip, but we had bad luck from the start and it stayed with us throughout the journey."

A pulley broke, killing one crewman. Sparing or dead-men were used with extreme difficulty to overcome sandbars and rapids, and when these techniques failed, the captain would call for volunteers to get in the river and drag a chain under the boat to dislodge obstructions. After spending two days grounded on an especially difficult sandbar, it was decided to cache several thousand dollars' worth of furs and buffalo hides on shore—a desperate measure. An immense herd of buffalo swimming across the river caused pandemonium and further delay. Some men pursued the animals in small life boats, while others chased the buffalo from shore. A man named Arnold was ambushed by Indians, scalped and mutilated. To the dismay of passengers, progress on many days tallied a scant five or six miles.

By the end of October, Napton feared the *Imperial* might become marooned in ice for the entire winter. He and several concerned passengers found an abandoned mackinaw partially entombed in the mud, and working the oars day and night, the improvised crew reached Yankton, South Dakota, and then took horses to Booneville, Missouri, reaching it exactly three months after Napton had left Bear Gulch. Later it was reported that the *Imperial* had been abandoned 150 miles above Sioux City, Iowa, and the passengers transported to Yankton in horse-drawn wagons.

Passengers and crew crowded into limited space made steamers incubators for diseases; smallpox and cholera from asymptomatic passengers would become virulent, causing panic and fatalities; spoiled food and contaminated water caused dysentery.

The passengers' plight was mitigated somewhat by the scenery of ever-changing wilderness and the sighting of vast herds of buffalo and antelope. Not uncommonly, the vessel would steam in among herds of swimming buffalo. The abundance of game converted rational men into a blood-thirsty mob. The open hurricane deck or any other open space provided a stable platform for shooting. The ensuing melee of killing and wounding was horrible. Many shot animals sank and were wasted; some were salvaged, providing fresh meat for passengers and crew. Journals recorded the excitement of passengers indiscriminately shooting buffalo from the decks of steamboats. A passenger wrote: "We are now evidently in buffalo country…. Soon afterwards we saw another big band of buffalo—thousands of them—crossing the river, going south and the boat was headed for them and struck about the middle of the herd. Then the wheel was reversed, in order to hold the boat amongst them, and everybody shooting with pistol, shotgun, or pistol…. Three or four cows were hauled aboard, and this ended the slaughter." (*Big Sky Journal*) When boats were tied to shore for the night, men would shoot buffalo, cut out the tongues and chunks of choice hump meat, and leave several hundred pounds of carcass to the wolves.

Women passengers, while in the minority, seemed to tolerate the emotional ups and downs of a voyage with alacrity. Occasionally captains were accompanied by their wives, who wanted to see the new frontier and experience river travel. It was incumbent that homesteaders take their wives and children to the frontier; breaking the soil and carving out a life on the prairie necessitated a family effort. These adventuresome women were given due respect and admiration for their ability to cope. Most women acclimated to their surroundings, adjusting to the ineptitudes of river travel. Mrs. Harriet Sanders, residing in Virginia City, Montana, brought her two small sons and her mother to Fort Benton via steamboat in 1866. In her journal she matter-of-factly reported, "Alarm of Indians. They have attacked two boats and killed one man."

As is often the case with human memory, passengers who boarded a steamer for the trip up the Missouri would let the difficulties and inconveniences fade. Many would retell their days of adventure, remembering the splendor of wild landscapes and animals, the thrill of standing at the rail feeling the timbers of the floating hotel vibrating beneath their feet, and the cacophony of sounds. The ever-present specter of a confrontation with "savages" was an adventure all its own.

Women passengers were rare in the early days of the steamboat era, but as mining towns grew and farmers headed to the region, more women took passage. In this photo a number of women grace the decks of the Josephine, *docked at Fort Benton in the 1880s.* MONTANA HISTORICAL SOCIETY RESEARCH CENTER PHOTOGRAPH ARCHIVES, HELENA, MONTANA.

Despite the difficulties and risks, the once-in-a-lifetime drama of riding the "Big Muddy" must have spawned feelings of participating in American history.

Today, adventurous travelers can see landscapes that those mid-nineteenth century travelers would recognize. The fading, late afternoon alpenglow turns sandstone cliffs from a deep orange to faint pink and then delicate purple. The buffalo are gone, but elk, mule deer, antelope, and wild sheep still survive in viable numbers. The author completed a multi-day canoe trip through the Upper Missouri River Breaks National Monument in Montana, and on more than one occasion had an unexpected surge of emotion, knowing the landscape appeared as unaltered as that witnessed by the early travelers. I formed a mental image of the smoke-belching, water-churning, metal-clanging monster coming around a river bend. Such vessels carried optimistic people that gambled everything to start a new life in the expanding American West.

CHAPTER 20

Steamboats and Native Americans: Trade and War

FROM THE EARLIEST CONTACTS with whites, the meeting of native peoples inhabiting North America represented a clash of cultures. The late 18th-century contacts with the French from the north and the Spanish from the south were intermittent and fleeting. The whites were non-threatening curiosities, strange men that introduced goods of unconceivable value: steel weapons, colorful glass beads, kettles, and strange food and drink. These items were eagerly sought and could be obtained by trading furs, easily obtainable and plentiful. The natives didn't realize that the white trappers were the vanguard of an influx of whites as numerous as leaves on a tree.

The tribes, seeing the first steamers belching their way up the Missouri River, were struck with a gamut of emotions. The first "fire canoes" combined thoughts of fear, dread, veneration, and wonder. Some considered steamers to be smoke-breathing serpents that "walked on water." They soon learned that these monsters brought volumes of goods greater than the trickle brought by pack strings of horses.

Three events altered to balance of power and soured Indian attitudes: diseases introduced by steamboats, the trading of alcohol, and the discovery of gold. These events created an attitude of defiance, changing the temporary equilibrium between the cultures.

The moral depravity caused by the illegal pedaling of alcohol and the introduction of diseases to which the natives had no resistance is well documented. Hundreds of years of incessant intertribal warfare, wars between the tribes and whites, and surviving in an unforgiving environment were trifling compared to the chronic, debilitating influences of alcohol and diseases. The Upper Missouri tribes were depopulated not by white soldiers, nor by superior weapons or military tactics, nor by the influx of land hungry immigrants, but by disease.

The American Fur Company's steamboat, the *St. Peters*, arrived at Fort Union on June 24, 1837. In the bowels of the steamboat lurked a pestilence that would pounce upon the Indians like a cloud of poison gas, spreading terror and death. Several of the steamboat's crew were infected with smallpox, but driven by an anticipated loss of profits, the company, well aware of the potential consequences, permitted the boat to land and conduct trade with the encamped Indians. For his part, the boat captain, reticent to ignore the falling water level as spring runoff subsided, did not want to strand his boat upriver by delaying commerce with the Indians until the disease had run its course among his crew. In addition, the effort and expense to move tons of goods up the Missouri had to be considered. And finally, the Indians were well aware of, and anticipated, the boat's arrival, and if the promised goods failed to be delivered, they would have considered it a perfidious act to cheat them.

The Assiniboine were the first to arrive at Fort Union. They traded buffalo robes for gunpowder and ball, sugar, coffee, and kettles. Within three days, the first Assiniboine showed signs of infection. The disease spread like wildfire, and the Indians fled onto the prairie, leaving trails of death.

The disease soon reached the Crow and Blackfeet nations, nearly exterminating the latter.

Smallpox arrived at different times at different locations. On June 15, 1837 the pox invaded the Mandan villages. The disease struck with a virulence never before seen in epidemics. In some villages it killed every person. The infected were stricken with massive skin eruptions, and the resulting viremia swept the person away in a matter of hours. Hundreds died each day.

Powerless to avert a disfiguring, painful death, many Mandans committed suicide by hanging or shooting themselves. Men shot their families before ending their own lives. Many simply wandered into the prairie to die alone. Women crawled among the bodies of children and husbands. The wind echoed with wailing and crying. The stench of death permeated the air for miles. The few Indians that survived were in a state of confusion, disbelief, and grief.

Most of the tribes of the Upper Missouri, to one degree or another, were eventually infected with the smallpox virus, resulting in appalling horror. Trader Alexander Culbertson was an eyewitness, visiting Fort McKenzie in 1837 where 500 lodges of the Blackfeet Nation had gathered in anticipation of trading for goods from a recently arrived steamboat. Culbertson warned the tribe not to come in and barter. The plague had infected the passengers and crew of the vessel and nearly everyone at the fort, overwhelming some but not all. (Over generations, Europeans had developed a degree of immunity to numbers of maladies that were deadly to the Indians).

Anxious to trade and ignorant of the deadly consequences of smallpox, the Blackfeet ignored the warning. Some thought it was a plot to deprive them of the trade goods they had come to depend on. Some historians have speculated that blankets contaminated with the virus were traded to the Blackfeet for the express purpose of eliminating that tribe's reign of terror across the Northern Plains, thus opening the territories to whites.

Because of a relatively short incubation period, sickness soon began to erupt in the tribe. Lacking an understanding, thinking a supernatural phenomenon was occurring, the tribe fled, attempting to leave behind what they couldn't comprehend. The rapacious virus traveled with them. Unburied dead bodies, abandoned lodges, and personal possessions littered the prairie like a string of evil. Incredibly, from 500 lodges, only two individuals survived.

There have been a number of mortality estimates suffered by the Upper Missouri tribes. One author estimated that 15,000 perished, about one-third of the total population, with some tribes nearly exterminated. Prince Maximilian personally witnessed the effects and wrote succinctly: "The mighty warriors are now the prey of the greedy wolves, and the few survivors, in utter despair, throw themselves on the pity of the whites, who, however, can do little for them. The vast preparations for the protection of the western frontier are superfluous; another arm has undertaken the defense of the white inhabitants of the frontier; and the funeral torch, that lights the red man to his fiery grave, had become the auspicious star of the advancing settler and the roving trader of the white race." (*The American Fur Trade of the Far West*, Vol. 2)

Eventually the tribes, especially the nomadic Sioux and Cheyenne who were less affected by disease, underwent a metamorphosis, finally understanding the reckless aims of the whites. The tribes began attacking steamboats, Army outposts, and vulnerable whites at every opportunity.

Carrying supplies, soldiers, and the wounded, steamboats helped the U.S. Army win the Indian Wars. Then some of the same boats transported the defeated tribes to reservations. In this photo the Helena, *docked at Bismarck, North Dakota, carries Sioux to the Standing Rock Agency in the Dakotas.* STATE HISTORICAL SOCIETY OF NORTH DAKOTA

The Yankton branch of the Sioux Nation were the most belligerent. Concealed in the brush and coulees, men would frequently shoot at river traffic, including steamboats laden with goods and passengers. Aware that steamboats held tons of coveted commodities, the Indians devised another cunning tactic by which buffalo robes were piled on the shore as if to solicit trade. An Indian, using any available means to accomplish his ends, would squat to his neck in the muddy water. The steamboat captain, thinking the water was neck deep, would approach, only to ground the vessel within range of shot and arrow.

Sioux raiders earned the name "pirates of the Missouri." Isolated wood hawks were especially victimized, and hunters, hired by the steamboat captain to supply fresh meat, were frequent targets. Crew members gathering wood or hooking ropes to trees or rocks to surmount rapids would be ambushed. The Teton band of Sioux preyed upon small groups of fur traders, confiscating entire stocks of goods. Traders doing business with the Sioux were at risk and, of necessity, were solicitous of the tribe.

The Sioux knew the well-armed steamboats were moving people and soldiers into their traditional lands. Therefore, steamboats were attacked, usually from an elevated vantage point where the channel of the river forced the boats near shore. The favored target was the wheelhouse, the top-most structure on a steamer, putting the captain at great risk. Bullets plinked off the metal plates that shielded the wheelhouse.

Steamers did not enjoy the luxury of an army escort while traveling up river, except in the immediate proximity of an established fort. However, most male passengers were armed, and these passengers, so inclined, would shelter at the vessel's railings and return fire, occasionally becoming casualties. Usually, the raids were of limited tenacity, doing marginal damage to the attacker and the attacked. At night, vessels were tethered to islands or anchored in midstream, and guards were posted.

The military campaigns against the Indians on the Upper Missouri essentially came to an end soon after the Custer massacre in 1876. Some isolated skirmishes occurred into the early 1880s, but the power of the U.S. Army broke the

Sioux and Cheyenne nations. The tribes were forced onto reservations, although a few members held out for a short period in Canada. All along the Upper Missouri, the Indians' mood turned to resignation. Ultimately, steamboats provided a final insult: crowds of Indian families were transported to reservations by the same steamboats that played major roles in their defeat.

In 1881 the Eclipse *(in the front), under the command of Captain Grant Marsh, was the flagship of a fleet of five steamboats that carried 3,000 Indians from the Yellowstone region to Standing Rock Agency in the Dakotas. From left to right, at the Bismarck levee circa 1880, there is an unknown steamboat, then the* Nellie Peck, Red Cloud, Gen. Charles H. Tompkins, *and the* Eclipse. MURPHY LIBRARY SPECIAL COLLECTIONS, UNIVERSITY OF WISCONSIN-LA CROSSE.

CHAPTER 21

Serving the Army

THROUGHOUT THE INDIAN CONFLICT, steamers played a pivotal role in defeating the tribes of the Northern Plains and thereby opening the intermountain west to colonization. After the Indian wars, in order to fulfill its obligation to protect the increasing flood of whites into the Upper Missouri, the United States Army depended on steamers to deliver annuities to the Indians and supply riverside forts with soldiers and supplies. From 1866 to 1876 the Army shipped more freight tonnage and personnel on the Missouri than any private company.

Steamboats became a lifeline to soldiers facing winter garrison duty on rations of hardtack, corn meal, and salt pork. They reliably delivered sugar, coffee, blankets, canned fruit, and clothing at the appointed time and place. Letters from home were causes for celebrations.

One can only speculate how fundamentally the settling of the northwest would have been altered had the Army not contracted steamer pilots to move vast quantities of supplies and soldiers. At a minimum, settlement and development of natural resources would have been delayed decades.

CHAPTER 22

Steamboat Wrecks and Accidents

INHERENTLY, STEAMBOATS WERE VICTIMS of any number of calamities due to their construction, weather phenomena, a pilot's miscalculations, and river hazards. Steamboat crews and passengers knew a certain lethality accompanied steamboat travel like a sinister, foreboding omen.

In 1834 the American Fur Company suffered a major economic setback when the *Assiniboine* wrecked and burned near the mouth of Heart River in North Dakota. On board were 1,100 packs of buffalo robes, each pack having 10 robes, and Prince Maximilian's zoological, botanical, and ethnological specimens—all lost.

May 17, 1849, had been a warm spring day in St. Louis. As evening dissolved into night, a warm, pleasant breeze blew upstream. A fire ignited deep in the hull of the steamer *White Cloud* anchored at a levee crowded with vessels, including steamboats loaded with merchandise for Fort Benton. The cause of the fire was undetermined: perhaps a drunken crewman tipping a kerosene lamp, coals in a failed boiler, a spark from a lighted pipe. No matter. The steamer's kiln-dried wooden framework ignited and the fire spread quickly, leaping to adjacent steamers and to warehouses and buildings along the waterfront. Before it was stopped, the fire destroyed 23 steamboats and 15 city blocks.

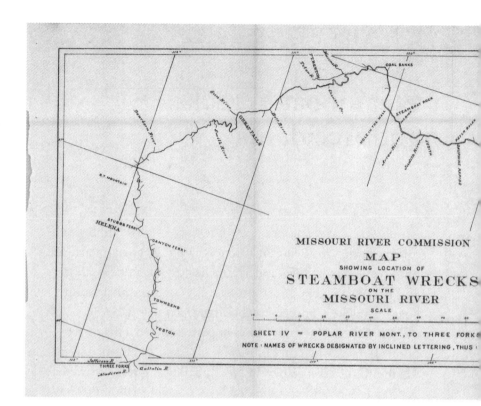

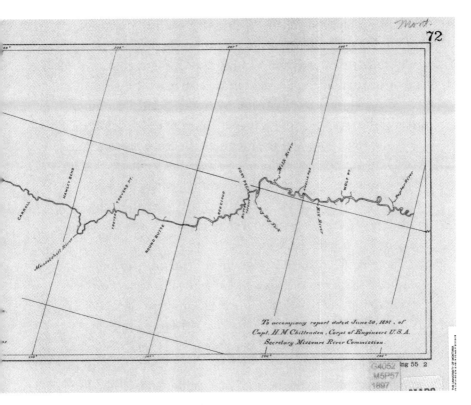

The life of an Upper Missouri River steamboat was short, about three years, because of multiple hazards on the ever-changing river. Most boats eventually wrecked on snags, sweepers, and rapids, or caught fire, or were blown apart when their boilers exploded, or collided with bridges downstream. Even tornados damaged some boats. But because the profit on one trip could pay for the boat's construction, crew, and much more, investors kept boat builders busy. This map, made in 1897, shows the locations of seven wrecks on the Missouri between Fort Benton and North Dakota. The wrecked steamboats were the Marion, Peter Balen, Trover, Red Cloud, Butte, Tacomy, and Amelia Poe. ARCHIVES AND SPECIAL COLLECTIONS, MANSFIELD LIBRARY, UNIVERSITY OF MONTANA.

Boiler explosions and the resulting fires were the most serious
and dreaded accidents. Demands from a determined pilot for
power to surmount a troublesome stretch of river could exceed
the structural capabilities of boilers. Such was the case in 1845
when the citizens of Hermann, Missouri, heard the ominous
roar of the exploding *Big Hatchie*. Thirty-five people lost their
lives. In 1861, a fire on the mountain boat *Chippewa* ignited
barrels of gunpowder, reducing the vessel to a raft of splinters.
The passengers and crew escaped death, having gone ashore in
great haste to escape the fire. In August 1854, a boiler explosion
killed the *Timour's* captain and clerk while the crew was taking
on wood near Jefferson City.

Pilots that remained upriver into September or pilots attempting to maximize profits by being the first reach Fort Benton in the spring risked grinding collisions with chunks of ice.
A river channel clogged with ice floes driven in unpredictable
directions by swirling currents presented considerable challenges. Pilots, from elevated wheelhouses, would alert roustabouts stationed at the bows. They would fend off the bergs
with steel-tipped poles. The most calamitous damage occurred
when rising water dislodged massive sheets of ice that the river
currents forged into a grinding, angular ridge several feet thick.
This wall of ice, pushed downstream by freshening currents,
resembled a glacier, crushing all in its path.

High winds stalked the Missouri River like an occult,
supernatural force. Forty-knot winds could appear with no
warning, pressing against the superstructure of a steamer and
spinning it out of control. Tornados, although uncommon,
were the most feared. In a few seconds the massive bulk of a
steamer could be reduced to a pile of rubble. In 1879, at Bismarck, North Dakota, a tornado tore off the upper decks of
the steamer *Montana*, flinging timbers several hundred yards.

Rocks submerged in rapids and logs anchored in the river bottom tore open hulls. They lay concealed beneath a few inches of opaque water. A jarring rumble deep in a vessel told of a strike. Water gushed into the holds, causing the vessels to list and not infrequently sink.

Rare but serious collisions with bridge abutments accounted for some steamers sinking into the river ooze. In 1867, a steamer careened out of control near Arrow Rock, Missouri, and smashed into an obstruction, causing the fire box heating the boiler to crash off its moorings, which then caused an explosion of boiling steam and fire. The vessel sank in less than an hour. In 1884 near St Charles, Missouri, the unfortunate *Montana* sank after the pilot misjudged a current and collided with the foundation of a railroad bridge. Some cargo and machinery was saved, but the steamer was never salvaged.

Because of the shallowness of the Missouri and the three-story height of a steamer, human causalities following a sinking were uncommon. At hearing the alarm bell, passengers would scramble to the high, hurricane deck, rarely getting their feet wet.

CHAPTER 23

Trying to Tame the River

THE PITFALLS OF NEGOTIATING the Upper Missouri frequently caused delays in servicing army forts and depots along the river. In some instances, supplies failed to arrive at all. Sagging soldier moral and intensifying Indian hostilities convinced the military to find a way to ameliorate the risks of sending vital supplies upriver. About 1870, motivated by a sense of urgency, radical thinking about the designs and uses of steamers brought about partial solutions.

In 1870, the only government agency capable of addressing the problems of enhancing safe and dependable travel on the Upper Missouri was the Army Corps of Engineers. Attacking the problems necessitated a two-prong approach: customizing existing steamboats to facilitate obstruction removal, and developing techniques for clearing obstructions. In some places the riverbed was altered by dredging sandbars or shoring up collapsing banks. Clearing obstructions proved particularly onerous because of the fluid, seasonal nature of sandbars and the deposit of newly uprooted trees with each spring's runoff. River improvement projects were never-ending. Surveyors were sent to identify and catalog hundreds of hazards. Channels through rapids were blasted with charges of dynamite; pervasive log jams were sawed and blasted; hundreds of hull-piercing logs were winched

In an effort to make the Missouri safer for steamboats, the U.S. Army Corps of Engineers retrofitted some steamboats into "snag boats" like the one shown here. Using powerful winches, they pulled fallen trees from the river. It was a never ending task of limited success.

out; precipitous riverbanks prone to collapse were identified and marked.

The converted, river-clearing steamboats were huge. The *Josephine* measured 178-feet and served as a floating work platform that moved from one project to another. The work boats were fitted with all manner of construction equipment: primitive cranes, heavy-duty steam-powered capstans, shovels, saws, axes, dynamite, winches, and thick chains and cables. There was a compliment of laborers, metal workers, carpenters, boiler men, and cooks. The main vessel was shadowed by a smaller steam-powered boat capable of working in shallow water and used to ferry laborers to riverside projects.

Workers were housed in onshore accommodations where available, or on board the large work boats, or on dilapidated scows towed behind the large workboat. Accommodating 100 men, the towed, barrack-type boats were simple canvas-covered wooden platforms. They were crowded, dirty, smelled bad, and provided a favorable environment for body and head lice. As in any army, the officers (here the engineers, some brought their wives) were designated the best accommodations, usually in spacious rooms in the stern of the vessel.

The technical means by which the engineers used to manage obstacles were innovative, many devised on site as the need arose. Still in use today in Montana as a means of channeling river water to irrigate hay fields is the technique of using walls constructed from river rocks or wood planking to channel water in a desired direction. The engineers designed dikes and piers angled into the river to prevent water from eroding or collapsing 20-foot-high riverbanks. To retard cave-ins, steamboats delivered millions of saplings that were cleverly woven into gigantic retaining walls.

In 1838, an innovative ship builder named Henry Shreve

devised a vessel capable of scooping in, through an opening in the bow, sunken tree trunks and attached roots. The tree and roots were winched on board and then disposed on shore. Shreve's clever design languished until resurrected by the Army Corps of Engineers in the late 1800s. Boats could lift the largest snags and pull them aboard with a steam-powered windlass. Such boats earned the nickname of "Uncle Sam's Toothpullers."

Attempting to clear the Missouri of impediments began in earnest with spring run-off. A never-ending deluge of logs, tree limbs, and roots, shifting sandbars, and collapsed banks proved insurmountable. No doubt, however, some serious accidents were prevented by the actions of the Army Corps of Engineers. Today, "Old Muddy" is a pale remnant of its former self. Multiple dams have, for the most part, tamed the river.

CHAPTER 24

A Golden Spike Sinks the Golden Era of Steamboats

EVEN THOUGH THE COMMERCIAL ENTERPRISE proved profitable for merchants, pilots, and boat builders, moving freight and passengers up and down the Missouri River on steamboats was inherently more expensive and time consuming than transport by rail. The driving of the golden spike at Promontory Point, Utah, on May 10, 1869, commenced a death struggle between steamboat travel and railroads. The insurmountable Rocky Mountains had been conquered. Ribbons of steel connected the east and west coasts. The degree of isolation that had kept the West from fully being exploited, evaporated. Ironically, the mastery of steam power by steamboat engineers laid the seeds of the steamboats' destruction. Steam harnessed in specialized boilers and pipes drove steel wheels along steel rails, carrying more quantities of freight and passengers over longer distances in less time than a steamer. The economic equation had morphed.

For a period, an uneasy rivalry existed between the railroad and Missouri steamboats. The rivalry eventually turned into a competitive struggle. Gradually, more lengths of track paralleled the river, reaching ports of call that had been serviced by steamers for decades. Merchandise carried by rail proved less costly to consumers and arrived in a timely fashion. Passengers traveled in more comfort and arrived at destinations weeks before steamers. Once the rails reached Fort Benton, the northern most river port, in 1887, the struggle ended. The Golden Age of the upper Missouri River steamboats was over.

Missouri steamers continued to provide some limited services, aiding in government projects and supplying quantities of bulky construction materials and livestock to isolated riverside forts and outposts. In 1889, the *F. Y. Bachelor* disgorged the last steamboat shipment of commercial freight at the Fort Benton levee. In time, the sight of a whistle-blowing behemoth frothing its way to the levee, its hold packed with the essentials of civilized society, faded in importance.

Railroads sank the steamboat era on the Upper Missouri. For hauling passengers and freight, railroads were cheaper, faster, and operated year-round. The F. Y. Batchelor, *shown here, was the last steamboat to make a commercial freight run to Fort Benton. The year was 1889.* OVERHOLSER HISTORICAL RESEARCH CENTER, FORT BENTON.

Bibliography

Abel, Annie, Heloise, *Tabeau's Narrative of Loisel's Expedition to the Upper Missouri,* University of Oklahoma Press, Norman, Oklahoma, 1939.

Adams F. Ramon, *The Book of the American West,* Bonanza Books, New York, N. Y., 1963.

Bradbury, John, *Travels in the Interior of America in Years 1809, 1810, and 1811,* Biblio Life, LLC, London 1819.

Capps, Benjamin, *The Indians,* 1973.

Crutchfield, James, A., *It Happened in Montana,* Falcon Press Publishing Co. Inc., Helena, Montana, 1992.

De Voto, Bernard, *Across the Wide Missouri,* Houghton Mifflin Co., Boston, Mass., 1947.

Denig, Edwin, Thompson, *Five Indian Tribes of the Upper Missouri,* University of Oklahoma Press, Norman, Oklahoma, 1961.

Ferris, W. A., *Life in the Rocky Mountains,* Old West Publishing Co., Denver, Co. 1940.

Fischer, Hank and Carol, *Paddling Montana,* Falcon Press Publishing Co. Inc., Helena, Montana, 1999.

Gildart, R. C., *Montana's Missouri River,* Montana Geographic Series, Montana Magazine, Inc., Number 8, Helena, Montana.

Haywood, Carl, W., *Sometimes Only Horses To Eat,* Stoney Dale Press, Stevensville, Montana, 2008.

Holmes, Kenneth, L., *Covered Wagon Women,* Vol. 1840-

1849, University of Nebraska Press, 1983.

Irving, Washington, *The Adventures of Captain Bonneville*, Binfords and Mert Publishers, Portland, Oregon.

Lee, C. M., (diary), Edited by Hampton, Duane, H., *Life and Death at the Mouth of the Musselshell Montana Territory*, 1868-1872, Stoney Dale Press Publishing Co., 2011.

Maximilian, Prince of Wied, Maximilian, *Prince of Wied's Travels in the Interior of North America 1843*, (Vol. 1), Applewood Books, Carlisle, Massachusetts.

Merck Veterinary Manual, 9th Edition, Merck and Co., Inc, Publisher, Whitehouse Station, New Jersey, 2005.

Monahan, Glenn., *Montana's Wild and Scenic Upper Missouri*, Northern Rocky Mountain Books, Anaconda, Montana, 1997.

Moulton, Gary, E., *The Definitive Journals of Lewis and Clark*, (Vol. 3) of the Nebraska Edition, From Fort Mandan to Three Forks, University of Nebraska Press, Lincoln, Nebraska, 1987.

O'Neil, Paul, *The Rivermen*, Time Life Books, Inc., New York, New York.

Petsche, Jerome, *The Steamboat Bertrand*, History Excavation and Architecture, National Park Service, Washington D.C., 1974.

Switzer, Ronald, R., *The Steamboat Bertrand and Missouri River Commerce*, University of Oklahoma Press, Norman, Oklahoma, 2013.

Thomas, David, H., *The Native Americans*, Turner Publishing, Inc. Atlanta, Georgia, 1993.

Walcheck, Kenneth, C., "Steamboat A'Comin," *Big Sky Journal*, Fly Fishing 2013, Vol. XX, No.1, J. D. Publishing LLC. February, 2013.

Weisel, George, F., *Men and Trade on the Northwest Frontier*, Montana State University Press, Missoula, Montana, 1955.

About the Author

ED WOLFF D.V.M. practiced veterinary medicine for 45 years before retiring to pursue a writing career. He has written three previous books, several essays in national periodicals, and described surgical techniques in veterinary literature. He is a passionate student of 19th century Montana history. He lives with his wife Annie in the beautiful Bitterroot Valley at the foot of the Bitterroot Mountains in western Montana. The couple travels throughout the United States backpacking, canoeing, and driving their camper into remote country. Ed is an accomplished oil painter, and during their travels Ed and Annie collect reference photos for his landscapes and wildlife paintings that he exhibits in his studio/gallery.

Montana History Books

*Montana 1864:
Indians,
Emigrants, and
Gold in the
Territorial Year*

*Montana 1889:
Indians,
Cowboys,
and Miners
in the Year of
Statehood*

*The Montana
Medicine
Show's Genuine
Montana
History*

*Adventure Tales
of Montana's
Last Frontier*

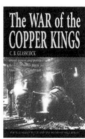
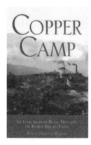
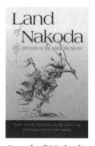
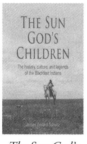

*The War of the
Copper Kings:
Greed, power,
and politics: the
billion-dollar
battle for Butte,
Montana, the
richest hill on
earth*

*Copper Camp:
The Lusty
Story of Butte,
Montana, the
Richest Hill on
Earth*

*Land of Nakoda:
From the tales
of the Old Ones
told to First Boy
with drawings by
Fire Bear*

*The Sun God's
Children: The
history, culture,
and legends of
the Blackfeet
Indians*

RIVERBEND
PUBLISHING

www.riverbendpublishing.com